CANTERBURY ARCHAEOLOGICAL TRUST OCCASION

WAINSCOTT
NORTHERN BY-PASS

ARCHAEOLOGICAL INVESTIGATIONS
1992–1997

by

Peter Clark, Jonathan Rady and Christopher Sparey-Green

with

Enid Allison, Ian Anderson, Robin Bendrey, John Cotter, Louise Harrison, Malcolm Lyne,
John McNabb, Nigel Macpherson-Grant, Ruth Pelling, Ian Riddler and Tania Wilson

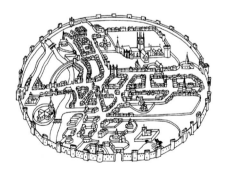

2009 Produced by Canterbury Archaeological Trust Ltd
Printed in UK by parkers digital press, Canterbury

The project was funded by Kent County Council

ISBN 978-1-870545-15-0
British Library Cataloguing-in-Publication Data
A catalogue record for this book is available from the British Library

Contents

List of figures

List of plates

List of tables

Summary

Between January 1992 and October 1997 watching briefs, evaluations and an excavation were conducted on the route of the Wainscott Northern Link or by-pass. This relief road was constructed over a distance of 5km from the junction of the A2 and M2, west of the original Medway crossing at Rochester north-east to the Four Elms roundabout on the A228 north of Wainscott.

Other than scatters of loose finds, little archaeological material was discovered over most of the route, but west of the Four Elms roundabout a multi-period settlement site was excavated. About 350 separate features and deposit sequences were examined, which may be divided into four periods.

Period 1 (prehistoric): a scatter of prehistoric ceramic and lithic material was recovered from the site and its immediate environs, the majority unstratified or residual and derived from nearby activity.

Period 2 (Roman): the main Roman structures comprised a small enclosure and an adjacent drying building (Structure 1) on a square plan *c* 3.5m wide externally. This was furnished with chalk-lined heating channels heated from a probably rebuilt furnace on the north side. Environmental evidence suggests the building had served as a malting or crop-drying oven. Large quantities of brick and tile wasters from the structure's fill indicated the presence of a nearby kiln site. Another fragmentary building (Structure 2) may belong to this period, in addition to a possible cremation burial. This layout was superseded by and enclosed within a larger ditched enclosure of at least 0.5 hectares with an entrance to the west. Pottery and coins from both phases can be dated to the late second and third centuries AD.

Period 3 (Anglo-Saxon): ditches representing an enclosure and its subsequent modifications (Enclosure 3) occupied the eastern part of the site during this period. A rectangular or 'bow-sided' building (Structure 3) approximately 14 by 6m, defined by shallow post-settings, was situated within the enclosure. A few metres to the west, traces of another structure (Structure 4), and perhaps other buildings were located. The structure was surrounded on south and east by a gully, probably an eaves-drip drain but perhaps also serving as another enclosure ditch. Both areas of occupation, which may be contemporary, were associated with groups of pits, some of which were used for the disposal of cess. Sparse occupation material of the Middle Anglo-Saxon period was recovered, environmental evidence suggesting small-scale agricultural activity.

Period 4 (medieval and post-medieval): parallel drainage or field boundary ditches and a ploughsoil containing eleventh- to twelfth-century material suggests agricultural activity in the succeeding period, perhaps part of an open field system. In the post-medieval period a substantial ditched field boundary or drain was cut across the site.

Acknowledgements

The evaluation, excavations and watching brief were all funded as part of the road construction costs through Kent County Council Highways, and thanks are due to Ron Martin of KCC Highways and to Lis Dyson of KCC's Heritage Conservation Group for facilitating the various stages of the project. The fieldwalk survey (1992) and early watching briefs of 1994 and 1995 were conducted by Alan Ward. The evaluation, which was carried out in appalling weather conditions in early January 1997, was supervised by Alan Ward, Simon Pratt and Tim Allen under the overall direction of Jon Rady, who also supervised the excavation of the same year. We would also like to thank all those who took part in the excavation, including Alison Denton who later assisted in compiling the archive.

The watching brief during road construction was principally undertaken by Jon Rady with assistance from Alan Ward and Adrian Murphy, and we would like to thank John Standing, general foreman of the main contractor McAlpines for his help during this phase and for supplying plant at the Four Elms roundabout excavation.

The present report was prepared for publication by Jon Rady, Christopher Sparey-Green and Peter Clark. The specialist contributors, both internal and external, are thanked for their assistance throughout and for their patience. Site drawings were prepared for publication by Peter Atkinson and finds drawings by Dominique Bacon, Will Foster and Beverley Leader. The report has been copy-edited by Jane Elder and prepared for print by Mark Duncan and Jane Elder.

The Four Elms roundabout can be seen north-west of centre in this aerial view. Photograph: Blom Aerofilms (24.7.95).

1

Introduction

Jonathan Rady and Christopher Sparey-Green

Archaeological work was carried out during the construction of a new by-pass to relieve congestion on the north-west side of the Medway conurbation (the Wainscott Northern Link). The road was located on the western side of the River Medway, extending from the existing junction of the A2 and M2 (TQ 695 695) north-east around the north-western side of Strood and Frindsbury to a point on the A289 north of Wainscott (TQ 751 713). The topography of the area is dominated by an east-north-east trending dry valley, originating near Cobham Park and following a sinuous course before turning south-east to meet the Medway at Whitewall Creek (Fig 1).

Field survey produced only limited results and the major part of this report is an account of the excavation of a multi-period site found at the northern end of the road, close to the Four Elms roundabout.

Site location, topography and history

The site is situated near the eastern edge of the present parish of Frindsbury Extra, north of Wainscott, itself now the northern edge of the suburban development of Frindsbury and Strood, north-west of the Medway river from Rochester. This section of the road scheme lay south east of Islingham Farm and east of the Royal School of Military Engineering.

Pl 1. The site, looking south-east. The ditches of Enclosure 3 are visible in the foreground.

1

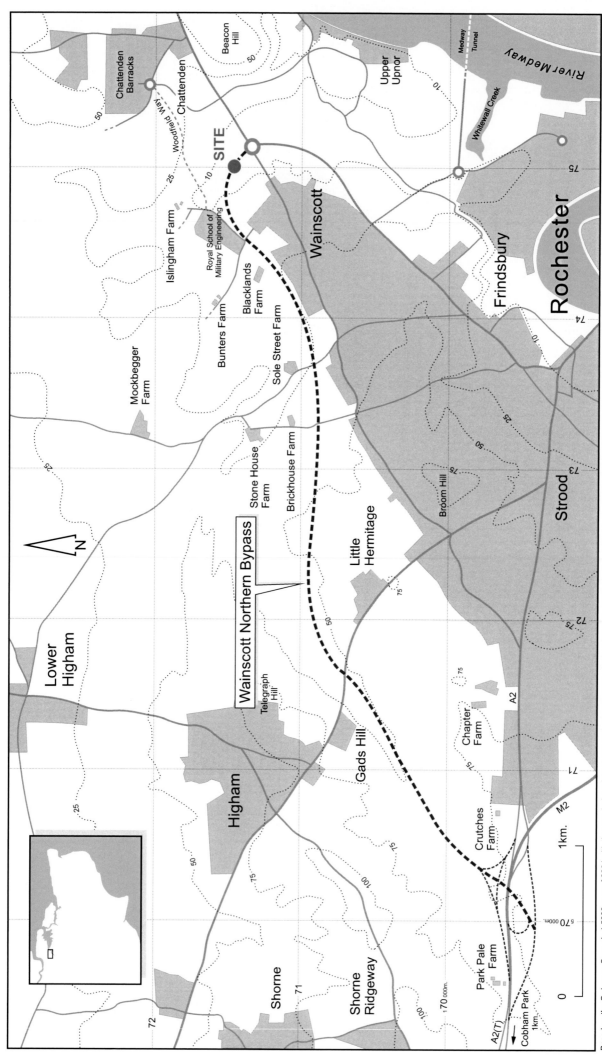

Fig 1. Site location.

Based on the Ordnance Survey's 1:5000 map of 2004 with the permission of the Controller of Her Majesty's Stationery Office. © Crown Copyright. Licence No. AL100021009

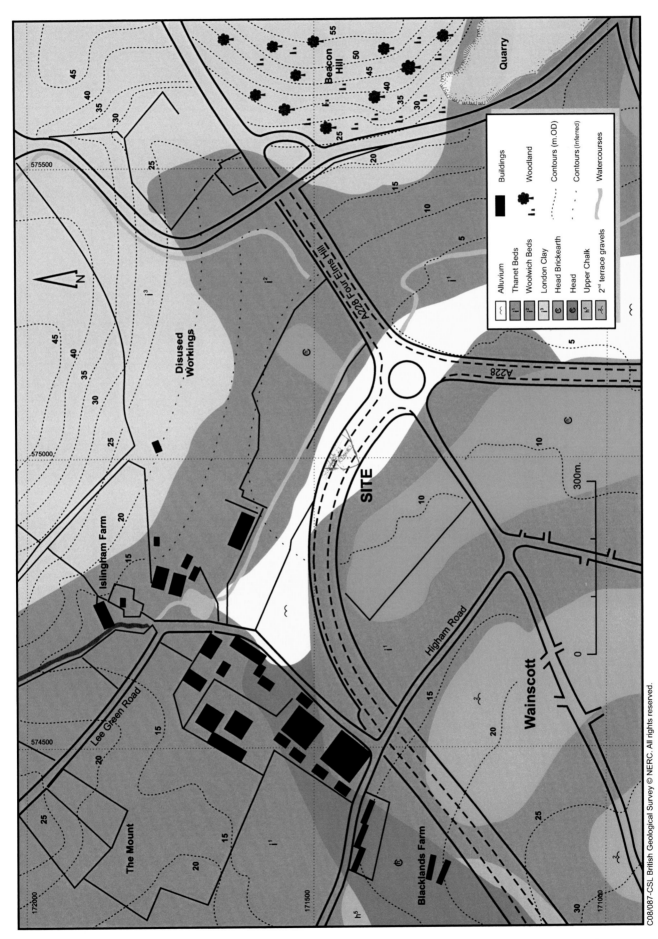

Fig 2. Local geology (based on the Geological Survey of Great Britain (England and Wales), sheet 272).

The excavated site lay at about +7m OD, close to the base of a valley which originates almost 2km to the north in Great Chattenden Wood and which leads a sinuous course southwards to join Chatham Reach at Whitewall Creek 2km to the south. A small stream follows the base of the valley and passes the site on the north-east side, following a course approximately parallel with and 70m north of the new road line. Beyond this stream is an arable field that on inspection in October 2000 yielded little sign of earthworks, variations in soil colour or finds that would have indicated that the site extended across the valley floor to the north-east. The excavated site, however, had proved to be sealed by a layer of alluvium or old ploughsoil so any extension of the site in this direction might be sealed beneath sterile soil.

To the west and south the land rises gently to a level of approximately 80m OD, close to the line of the A2 almost 4km distant. On the north, east and south-east, however, a series of small, steep-sided hills adjoin the valley and separate it from the main river channel. The nearest of these, above Woodfield Way has had its lower slopes considerably disturbed by excavations associated with the Royal School of Military Engineering. The hill to the east, Beacon Hill, rises to 59m OD and provides a good view east from Upnor Reach to the outer part of the Medway estuary. This hill was used as a beacon site in recent times but could have served as a lighthouse or guiding point for river traffic approaching Rochester in earlier periods. This point on the river would also form the lowest landing point above the marshes of the lower estuary.

Geology and natural resources

The geology of the by-pass route is varied, but is dominated by 'head' deposits, generally brickearth type clays, and outcrops of Thanet Beds, mostly sand or sand and pebbles. The area of the site is shown as Alluvium on the Geological Survey of Great Britain (England and Wales) Sheet 272, bounded to north and south by Thanet Beds (Fig 2). These deposits overlie Upper Chalk, which also outcropped along the route. The alluvium and nearby contours clearly indicate the presence of an ancient relict watercourse, following a meandering course towards the River Medway to the east. Outcrops of Head Brickearth also exist immediately to the north-east, and more extensively to the south and south-west. The higher ground to the north also shows evidence for a number of subsidiary streams flowing down towards the main valley.

The subsoil here is reworked brickearth, deposited as a result of ancient river activity, and containing mammalian remains of possible Upper Pleistocene date. The underlying well-sorted and rounded gravels and laminated sandy loam horizon suggest an alluvial and not a colluvial origin for these units (Pratt and Newstead 1997). The upper horizon

(1000) was part of an extensive level redeposited over the valley floor, which had probably accumulated due to long term agricultural use.

The major geological deposits cut by the valley at Wainscott are Thanet, Blackheath and Woolwich Beds but areas of Brickearth occur on both sides of the valley within a radius of 200m. Extensive areas of London Clay also occur to the north and the Upper Chalk is accessible both lower down the valley and further up to the south-west.

Previous discoveries in the area

Few sites are known in the immediate vicinity of the Four Elms roundabout and finds were generally rare along the line of the road scheme.[1] The only site subject to previous investigation lay at the opposite end of the road scheme from the Four Elms roundabout site. At a point 1.5km west of the junction with the A2 in Cobham a Roman villa and an Iron Age occupation site have been identified 300m south of the line of Watling Street (Tester 1961). The majority of the recorded sites are clustered to the east, closer to the bridgehead of the Medway crossing at Rochester but a number can, however, be identified close to the northern end of the road line, within the northern part of the parish of Frindsbury Extra and west towards Higham and Shorne.

Ring-ditches visible on air photographs suggest the sites of Bronze Age barrows, four being known in the area to the west of Wainscott (Kent SMR, sites TQ77 SW27 and TQ77 SW44). Two cremation burials from the foot of the hill 400m north of the site date from the late Bronze or early Iron Age (Jessup 1930, 123–4). Further afield, an Iron Age coin hoard has been recovered 3km to the west close to Higham and an enclosure of Iron Age type has been identified north of the village (Kent SMR, site TQ77 SW45). A cremation burial is known within the village and cropmarks of two inter-linked rectangular enclosures, on the lower slopes of Telegraph Hill on the outskirts of the village (TQ 717 710) may mark another settlement of Iron Age or Roman date.

The major sites of the Roman period lay 2km to the south of Wainscott, close to the Roman road and river crossing to Rochester. Major buildings, presumably villas, are known on the spit of land in the sharp bend in the river at Frindsbury and close to the bridgehead at Strood (Arnold 1889; Taylor 1932, 115–6). The Frindsbury site is notable for the presence of a lead coffin, presumably from the owner's family burial plot (Arnold 1887, 189). Other burials dating both to the Roman and Anglo-Saxon periods occur near the road line (Taylor *et al* 1932, 169–70; Vallance 1920; Meaney 1964, 138, Strood III). A series of pits close to Strood Church and the western bridgehead may have been domestic but their rich contents could suggest a ritual function (Green 1976, 229).

The discovery, however, of a Roman amphora and iron lamp, 1km south-west of the present site, is noteworthy

---

1. In the following account principal published references are given where they exist, otherwise the designation under the County Sites and Monuments Register (SMR) is quoted; in a few cases where sites have only recently been identified only the National Grid Reference is given.

because of the unusual nature of the objects and their location on the nearest high point in that direction (Kent SMR TQ77 SW15). This find would suggest a high status burial placed in a prominent location close to an important settlement; finds of Roman pottery and deposits of ash and scattered tile debris at two points 1 km to the west might derive from such a settlement or from an industrial site (Thornhill and Payne 1980, 379–80). Cropmarks west of the site and north-west of Blacklands and west of Bunters Farm may result from pit digging, the irregularity of the 15 and 20m contour in this area supporting the existence here of disturbances in the upper, western branch of the valley (Kent SMR TQ77SW39 and TQ77SW42). The geology here is described as Head while the higher ground nearer the site is covered in Head Brickearth.

Documentary and topographic sources

Wainscott does not figure in *Domesday* or early charters and is likely to have been a small settlement within the parish of Frindsbury. The name derives from OE *waegn* (cart) and OE *cot* (cottage) (Wallenberg 1931, 230). From the entries for *Domesday* and *Domesday Monachorum*, Frindsbury was held by the Bishop of Rochester and was a fairly extensive parish of approximately 2000 acres (*c* 810 hectares). There was land for fifteen ploughs and a very limited area of meadow and woodland, a church and only a single mill.

Field survey and evaluation

Initial works commenced with a fieldwalk survey in 1992 followed by watching briefs in 1994 and 1995 on the diversion of gas mains prior to the major construction work (Ward 1992; 1994a; 1994b). Thereafter evaluation of virtually the entire route was carried out with generally negative results other than providing useful data on the geoarchaeology (Pratt and Newstead 1997). The majority of finds consisted of scatters of worked flint or of post-medieval pottery and peg tile, with a more significant lithic assemblage coming from Park Pale Farm (TQ 698 697 centred). Another significant find was a biface of Middle Pleistocene age, found unstratified on the surface during fieldwalking (TQ

Pl 2. The site during machine stripping, looking east.

7043 6983). However, a watching brief in 1997 during road construction discovered a previously unrecognised site at the northern end of the road line. Stripping of subsoil deposits west of the Four Elms roundabout revealed scatters of pottery, worked flints and a number of features, which prompted a formal excavation to be undertaken (Rady *et al* 2000).[2]

The Four Elms roundabout

With the agreement of KCC Heritage and Highways and the contractors, an area of approximately 5500m, was stripped by machine and cleaned by hand at TQ 7505 7140, extending up to the northern boundary of the easement but not including the line of an electricity cable and a haulage road (Fig 3). A scatter of features revealed in drainage work on the northern edge of the main excavation area was not fully investigated but showed that the site extended beyond the main area. Excavation of this site was necessitated by the anticipated level of machine disturbance during construction, fieldwork from May to July 1997 being followed by a further, unproductive, watching brief.

2. At about the same time, metal detectorists, working without permission within the road easement, made some significant discoveries both at this site and to the south. A presumed disturbed hoard of Bronze Age socketed axe heads was apparently located, during or just after the topsoil strip, immediately east of Blacklands Farm (TQ 7426 7118). The exact circumstances of this discovery are uncertain, but despite repeated examination of this area during topsoil stripping and ground reduction, no evidence for ancient activity was observed. It seems likely therefore, that the objects, if indeed they did originate here, were part of an isolated scattered hoard. Rochester Museum holds a set of photographs which are believed to show objects from the hoard. One of the finders retains part of the hoard, along with other Bronze Age finds, which he has shown to the Finds Liaison Officer for Kent. The Rochester Museum photographs appear to show two distinct groups of finds; one features eight socketed axeheads, a hafted knife and two copper alloy fragments (possibly parts of socketed axes). The other photograph depicts a larger group, which corresponds to the finder's collection seen by the Finds Liaison Officer. This features four complete socketed axeheads, eight socketed axehead fragments, one spearhead fragment, one hafted knife fragment, two sword or rapier blade fragments, another fragment that may be part of a spearhead, and twenty-two or twenty-three fragments of copper 'bun' ingot, including some very large fragments which may represent a single, complete, ingot. Unfortunately it is unclear from the photographs whether any of the objects appear in both images, although it appears that they do not. It is therefore impossible to say which objects relate to the Wainscott hoard and which to other finds. All of the material in the pictures is typical of late Bronze Age metal hoards from the South-east, dating to *c* 1000–800 BC. A number of such hoards have been recorded via the Portable Antiquities Scheme in recent years along the tributaries of the Medway.

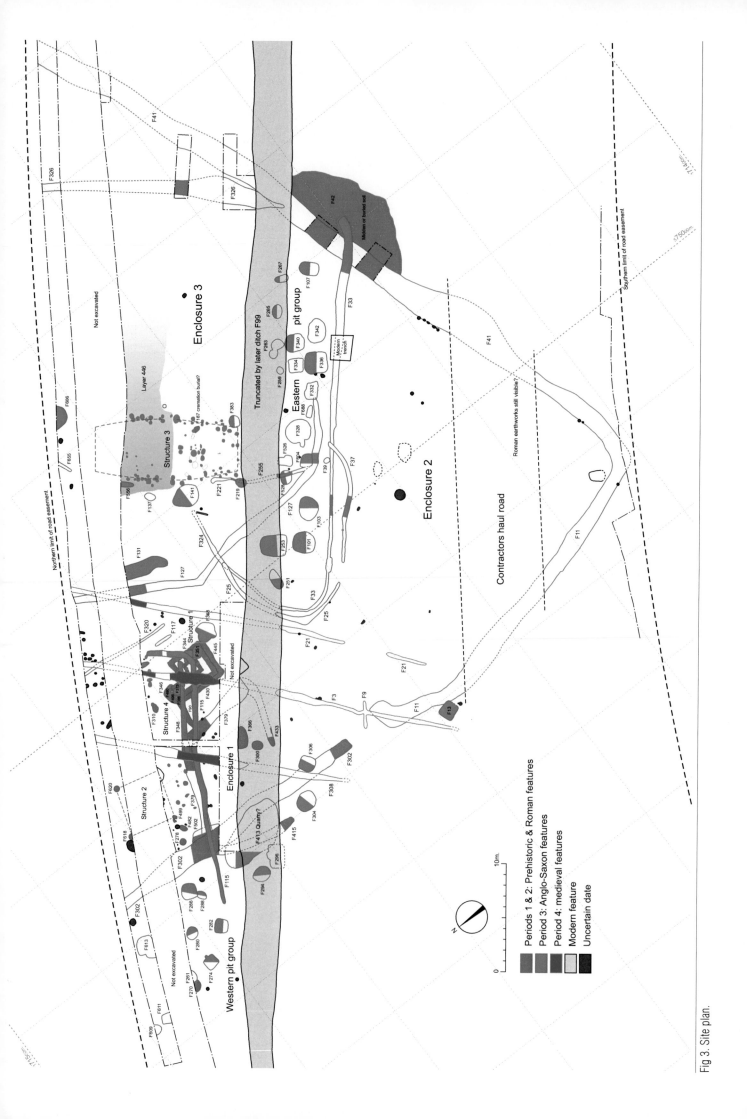

Fig 3. Site plan.

Western pit group

Not excavated

Structure 2

Enclosure 1

Structure 4

Structure 1

Enclosure 3

Not excavated

Northern limit of road easement

Layer 446

Structure 3

F187 cremation burial?

Truncated by later ditch F99

Eastern pit group

Modern or buried soil

Modern trench

Enclosure 2

Contractors haul road

Roman earthworks still visible?

Southern limit of road easement

F413 Quarry?

Periods 1 & 2: Prehistoric & Roman features
Period 3: Anglo-Saxon features
Period 4: medieval features
Modern feature
Uncertain date

N

0   10m.

F326 F41 F326 F606 F655 F131 F127 F320 F117 F310 F348 F344 F351 F445 F379 F366 F300 F433 F306 F302 F308 F304 F415 F296 F294 F115 F302 F352 F280 F288 F286 F270 F261 F274 F611 F609 F613 F620 F618 F499 F482 F502 F278 F379 F42 F267 F107 F33 F285 F263 F259 F342 F340 F334 F336 F332 F688 F328 F526 F494 F255 F221 F219 F141 F137 F556 F383 F103 F101 F253 F251 F127 F528 F39 F37 F33 F25 F21 F21 F3 F9 F11 F11 F13 F41 F430 F373 F346 F324 F25 F568

17150m 17450m 7750m

2
The Excavation

Jonathan Rady and Peter Clark

The bulk of the archaeological features were contained within an area of about 2200m², with about 700 separate contexts being recorded to varying levels of detail. These contexts comprised about 370 cut features and their fills, twenty-three layers and seven masonry walls. While approximately 70 per cent of the features were sample excavated and 6 per cent were completely excavated a further 24 per cent, mostly scattered post-holes, were only summarily recorded in plan and described briefly.

An east–west aligned post-medieval drainage ditch had removed part of the site while two strips occupied by a haulage road and a high-voltage electricity cable remained unexcavated.

Four periods of activity could be identified, based on dated finds and stratigraphic relationships. In many cases, both a lack of dating evidence for individual features and the absence of physical relationships between them means that the following phasing must depend in part on apparent associations or relative dispositions of features. The periods are designated as below:

Period 1: prehistoric
Period 2: Roman
Period 3: Anglo-Saxon
Period 4: medieval and post-medieval

Period 1: prehistoric

A considerable quantity of prehistoric ceramic and lithic material was recovered, much of this being unstratified or incorporated in the fill of later features. The lithic material was probably of late Neolithic or early Bronze Age date, perhaps indicative of domestic activity nearby during this period.[3] Around thirty sherds of pottery of middle Bronze Age date were also recovered, mostly small worn sherds from residual contexts, apart from a group of medium-sized

sherds from a pit (F270; Fig 4) in the north-western corner of the site. Only part of the curving south-western side was exposed, but it was at least 1.1m broad and 0.3m deep, the side sloping steeply. The pottery derived from its fill of silty-clay (269), which also contained fragments of burnt flint, daub, charcoal and part of a quernstone.

Period 2: Roman

The first substantial evidence for *in situ* activity dates from the Roman period and mainly comprised two successive enclosures and a masonry structure; few other features could be positively ascribed to this phase (Fig 4).

Pits

Two features appear to be slightly earlier than the main phase of Roman occupation on stratigraphic or artefactual grounds. Pit F278, 0.65m in diameter and 0.23m deep, with

Pl 3. Feature F278 with *in situ* pottery vessel. Scale 30cm.

---

3. Sub-contractors also recovered fragments of a mammoth tusk during trenching near the site. Although the precise location and depth of this find is not known, it may have been derived from fluvial levels associated with an old watercourse. Other fragments of very degraded bone tissue were recovered during the watching brief from depths of at least 2m in this area, but there was no associated lithic evidence.

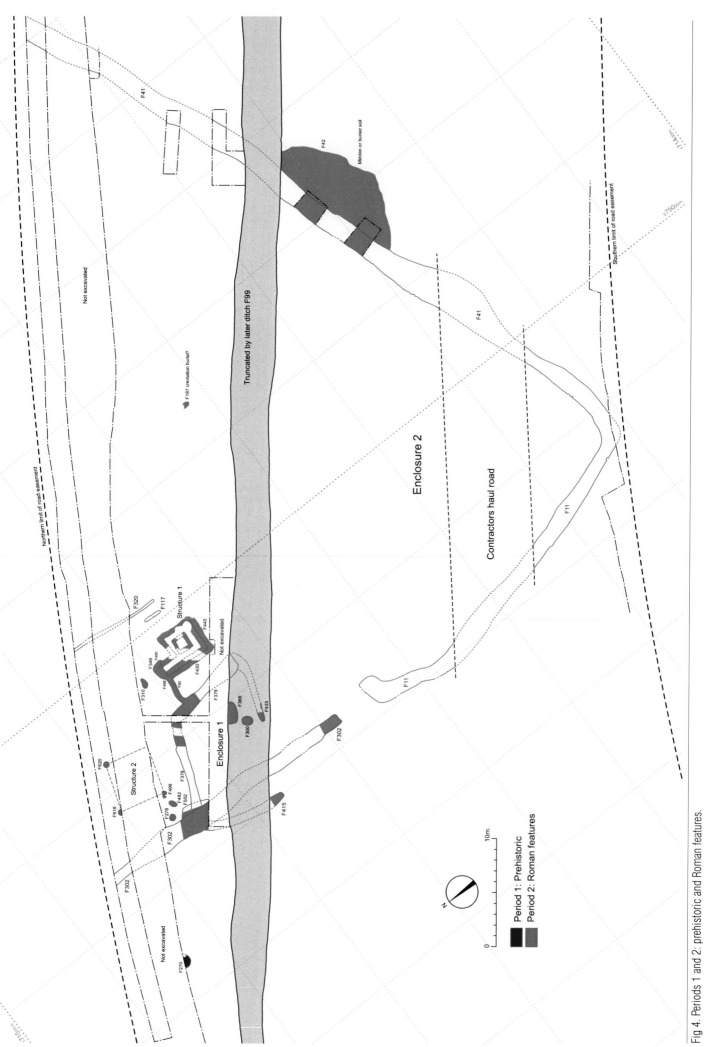

Fig 4. Periods 1 and 2: prehistoric and Roman features.

steep sides and a rounded base contained the fragmentary base of a North Kent Shell-tempered storage jar dated to *c* AD 50–170. The lower wall of the vessel, minus its base, was set upright, closely fitting within the feature (Pl 3). The vessel was filled with silty-clay (277) containing rare charcoal, daub, iron and decayed bone. Sherds of third-century pottery were also recovered. The jar would suggest a date for the feature prior to AD 150/170, but the absence of exclusively second-century pottery from the site as a whole, and the associated third-century ceramics suggest that the jar was already old when placed in the pit (p 41).

Immediately to the south of F278 was a truncated pit F502, at least 2.5m broad and 0.75m deep with steep sides and a flat base. It was filled with silty-clay or redeposited brickearth (501), containing some carbon, burnt flint and pottery of third-century date. It was cut by the ditch of Enclosure 1 (Figs 4 and 10).

Enclosure 1

An enclosure ditch formed an irregular quadrilateral about 11m by 8m, with a broad entrance on its southern side (Enclosure 1; Fig 4). Only short sections of the four sides were traced, formed by ditches F379, F415 and F433. There were few traces of associated features within the enclosed area.

The east and north sides were best preserved and comprised a steep V-cut ditch (F379) between 0.7 and 1.1m wide and 0.7m deep (Fig 7).

The west side of the enclosure had been heavily truncated; only a ditch terminal (F415) at the south-west corner survived, 0.89m wide and 0.15m deep, its sides sloping gently to a flat base.

The south side of the enclosure had also been heavily truncated; all that survived was the butt end of a ditch (F433), 7.5m to the east of ditch terminal F415. This was 0.60m wide and 0.10m deep, with sides sloping steeply to a flat base. It yielded a few sherds of a mid second- to third-century jar.

Few features can be associated with the use of Enclosure 1. A group of post-holes (F247, F298, F661, F663, F665,

F667 and F669; not illustrated), between 0.25 and 0.40m in diameter lay within its boundaries, but were not excavated. They were presumably structural, but no obvious structural plan could be discerned.

Lying within the south-eastern angle of Enclosure 1 was feature F366, a pit about 2m long by at least 0.9m broad and *c* 0.35m deep. It was filled with silty-clay (365), which contained a few sherds of Roman pottery of possible third-century date.

One other feature, (F300) situated near the south side of Enclosure 1, may originate in this period, but the dating evidence is ambiguous and an Anglo-Saxon origin is just as likely. The feature is described on p 27.

Structure 1

Lying about 2.5m east of Enclosure 1 was a masonry building (Structure 1), about 3.5m square, comprising a square central chamber enclosed within a concentric outer wall (Figs 5 and 6).

The building was set in a construction pit (F682), about 0.6m deep, with vertical sides and a flat bottom; the southern and western traces of this cut appear to have been removed by a possibly later drain (p 12).

The outer wall of the building (F83) was constructed of chalk blockwork bonded with puddled clay, generally about five courses high, with a rubble core of smaller chalk fragments and flint forming a square, each side measuring 3.55m externally. It was approximately 0.5m thick and around 0.5m high; the corners were reinforced at the base by irregular quoins of brickwork, one or two courses high and up to 0.9m by 0.45m square. The internal face of the wall sloped back, probably as a result of erosion rather than as a deliberate battered construction. Later alterations to the structure had substantially truncated the north-west corner of the building; no evidence for the original arrangement survived here, though the primary course of a brickwork quoin clearly marked the original corner of the structure at this point.

Set centrally on the southern side was a gap 1.13m wide and recessed 0.10m below the level of the external ground

Pl 4. Structure 1, partially sealed by old topsoil (82). Medieval ditch F3 can clearly be seen cutting through the building. Looking south. Scale 30cm.

Pl 5. Structure 1, looking north-east. Scale 2m.

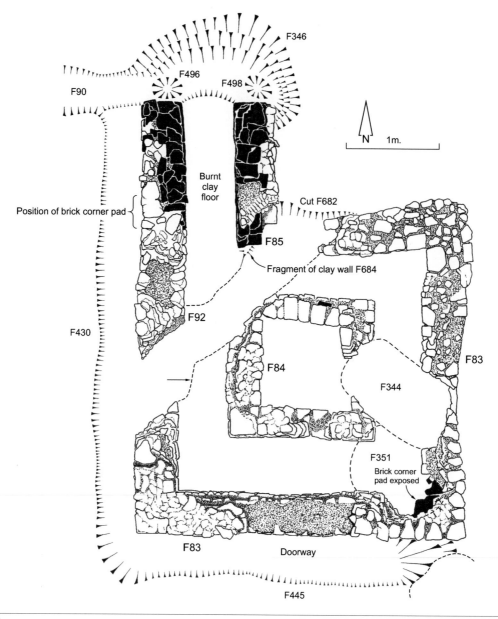

F346

F496

F498

F90

N   1m.

Burnt clay floor

Cut F682

Position of brick corner pad

F85

Fragment of clay wall F684

F92

F430

F84

F83

F344

F351
Brick corner
pad exposed

F83

Doorway

F445

Fig 5. Structure 1.

surface, presumably marking the position of a doorway. A layer of puddled clay on its surface may have been the bedding for a stone threshold, later removed.

Set within the outer wall was a slighter internal wall (F84), forming a square concentric with the outer walls, each side measuring about 1.3m externally. It was constructed of chalk blockwork bonded with puddled clay, generally about five courses high, with a rubble core of smaller chalk fragments and flint. The wall was about 0.32m thick and 0.45m high and enclosed a slightly raised platform of natural at the centre of the building. The outer face was well finished, and, where best preserved, raked back; the interior face, conversely, was slightly corbelled. The structure possessed no footings, but was built off the natural subsoil base of the construction pit. The intervening space between the inner and outer face of the flue was approximately 0.50m wide and

was floored by the surface of the natural (burnt in places) or patches of chalk dust or trample (685).

Insertion of stoke-hole and flue

Part of the external wall of Structure 1 was cut away at the north-west corner for the insertion of a masonry flue, consisting of two parallel walls (F85 and F92) each nearly 0.5m wide, 0.55m apart and extending about 1m from the northern wall of the structure. They were constructed mostly of complete roofing tiles (*tegula*) in about eleven courses, bonded with puddled clay, overlain by, or mixed in parts with, chalk masonry. This feature probably replaced and destroyed an original, shorter furnace that did not extend beyond the northern wall of Structure 1. On the western side, a cut (F91) through wall F92 indicated that about 0.6m of the

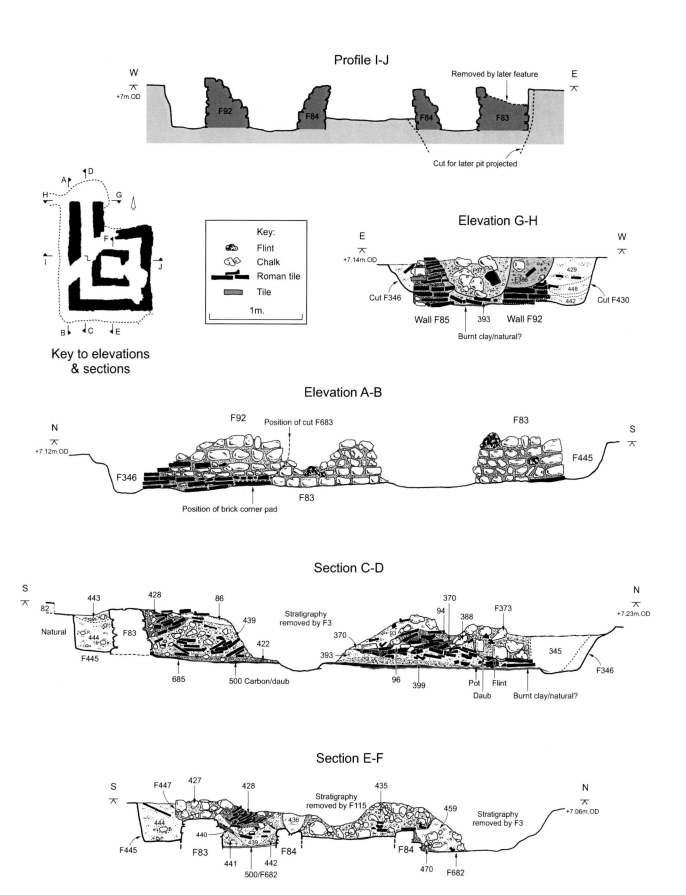

Fig 6. Elevations and sections through Structure 1.

Pl 6. Structure 1, detail of corner brick pad. Scales 1m and 30cm.

original wall had been removed, indicating that the new build here (F92) was just over 1.5m long. The putative junction of the new eastern wall F85 and the original northern wall of Structure 1 had been destroyed by later truncation. The inside faces of the flue walls were heavily fired, as was the natural clay floor. One dish rim fragment found within the matrix of the flue walls suggests that they were constructed in the early third century (p 38).

Pl 7. Structure 1 and associated drainage system, looking west. Scales 1m and 2m.

At the northern extremity of the flue was a steep-sided oval pit F346, 1.8 by 1.3m broad, its floor set at a similar depth (or just lower) to that of the flue. Signs of burning at its base suggest it had served as a stoke-hole. Two shallow depressions (F496 and F498), between 0.2 and 0.3m in diameter and around 20mm deep were set in the floor of the pit, flanking the line of the flue.

Abutting the southern end of flue wall F85 was a remnant of clay walling F684, heavily truncated by later features, leaving a triangular stub measuring about 200 by 200mm. It had the same alignment as the flue wall, and possibly represents the remains of a clay wall built to divide the flue structure from the rest of Structure 1, bridging the gap between the north-western corner of the inner wall, F84 and the southern end of F85.

Drainage

The structure appears to have suffered drainage problems; it was provided with an external drain (F430/F445), with a near vertical side, about 0.4m wide and 0.5m deep, running along the southern and western walls of the building and the western side of the extended flue. The drain then turned westward (F90), running for about 3m before discharging into the eastern side of Enclosure 1 (F379). The OD levels at the base of the cut(s) clearly showed a downward slope from the south-east corner of Structure 1 into the Enclosure 1 ditch.

Use, disuse and abandonment

Lying on the floor of the channel between the inner and outer walls of Structure 1 and the north-western flue was a deposit of grey-black silty ash (500), with inclusions of carbon, tile, daub and one pottery fragment. It was between 5 and 120mm deep, being thickest where it abutted the walls. It was overlain in the area of the flue by a dark grey brown silty ash (399) with inclusions of carbon, daub, flint pebbles, small fragments of chalk and pottery. This carbon layer probably originated from burning in the flue area and stoke-hole (F346), and had been raked, or otherwise spread into the rest of the building. These levels probably represent primary deposits related to the use of Structure 1 and both contained grain, chaff and weed seeds (pp 66-67).

Following the deposition of these layers of ash, the north-western flue appears to have collapsed or have been demolished. Overlying the ash (399) and lying between the flue walls F85 and F92 was a 0.3m thick layer of medium to large fragments of tile (393), set in a loosely compacted matrix of silt and burnt clay. This in turn was overlain by a 0.10m thick layer of silty-clay (388), with inclusions of hewn chalk blocks and daub. These deposits may partly represent debris from the collapse of the flue roof.

With the destruction of the flue, Structure 1 appears to have been abandoned; the channel between the main walls of the building (F84 and F83) and the collapsed flue itself were infilled with a sequence of silty-clays (441, 440, 442, 439, 470, 459, 428, 370, 96, 94, 93 and 86), with inclusions of chalk, carbon, daub, tile, and pottery, representing both collapse of the superstructure of the building and deliberate dumping. One dump (428) consisted almost exclusively of large fragments of tiles.

Only a small quantity of pottery was recovered from the levels within the building, with the lower fills providing just one sherd, which can only be dated generally to *c* AD 50–250 and the upper yielding three sherds of probable third- to early fourth-century date. The deposits within the flue contained slightly more material of similar date including three large fresh sherds of a Thameside greyware jar which is likely to post-date AD 270.

Outside the structure, the drain along the southern and western sides (F430/F445) was infilled, in addition to the now defunct stoke-hole (F346), the east–west drain (F90) and the eastern ditch of Enclosure 1 (F379). The sequence of fills appeared contiguous throughout this series of cuts, suggesting they were all open and infilled contemporaneously. At the base of enclosure ditch F379 and the east–west drain F90 was a silty-clay (394/423) with inclusions of daub, charcoal, tile, pottery and a single third-century coin (FN 731). Above this was a layer of charcoal (422/431), with occasional fragments of daub, which extended from the enclosure ditch through east–west drain F90 into F430. Above this was a deposit of clay and silty-clay (444/448) in drain F430/F445 adjacent to the walls of Structure 1. This was sealed by an extensive layer of silty-clay (378/443/345/429 and 89), with fragments of chalk, daub, pottery and bone that formed the final fill of all these interconnected cuts. It would appear that most of these deposits developed through natural silting process rather than deliberate backfilling, though debris from the collapsing structure had been incorporated during their formation. The intervening carbon layer was probably derived from the firing of the structure. The levels also suggest that the ditch of Enclosure 1 was allowed to become infilled at the same time as the demise of Structure 1, perhaps suggesting a functional link between them.

The lower fill of this drain provided freshly broken sherds of late second- to third-century pottery, while the upper fill yielded a slightly larger assemblage of broadly third- to early fourth-century types and including fragments from a beaker also found in the fills of the stoke-hole. The contiguous infills of drain F90 and the Enclosure 1 ditch F397 all contained similarly dated ceramics, suggesting that Structure 1 and its associated complex of drains had been abandoned by AD 270 or slightly after.

Late in this sequence of collapse and dump deposits, and post-dating the infilling of the drains, was a robbing cut F447, set over the centre of the southern wall of Structure 1 and presumably dug to retrieve the stone threshold of the earlier door. It was infilled with clay mixed with chalk blocks and large fragments of flint (427).

Associated features

The surrounding area contained several post-holes, pits and gullies, some of which might be contemporary with Structure

1 (Fig 4). Feature F310 lay 2.5m north of, and directly in line with, the flue of the drying building. This feature consisted of an irregular oval scoop containing dark silt, charcoal and occupation material, capped by large fragments of Roman tile, the finds including quantities of animal bone, daub and Roman pottery of late second- to third-century type. It could have served as a hearth during the use of Structure 1.

Two narrow gullies (F117 and F320), lay to the east of Structure 1 and set on the same axis, the former 2m from the east wall, the latter 3m. Gully F117 was 1.8m long and 0.3m wide with rounded ends. Gully F320 had a rounded terminal to the south and was traced for at least 9m, the northern end lying beyond the limits of excavation. Neither was excavated but the common alignment suggests that they may be associated and had perhaps served as a boundary or as part of an ancillary building associated with Structure 1. Many of the post-holes in the vicinity cannot be dated. A row of unexcavated post-holes, F119, F121, F123 and F322, ranging in diameter from 0.15 to 0.40m, approximately parallel to the southern end of the gully F320 might have been associated with it on spatial grounds.

Pl 8. Structure 1, construction of flue wall D85, looking south. Scale 30cm.

Structure 2

Structure 2 was represented by a group of three flint post-pads, F499, F618 and F620, identified on either side of the unexcavated strip north of Enclosure 1 (Fig 4). Of these features only F499 was excavated, this feature consisting of a shallow scoop 0.55 by 0.40m and 0.04m deep filled with flint nodules. The similarity and position of the three features, set 4.5m apart in an L-shape suggested they formed part of a four-post setting, the missing base lying within the undug ground. Their alignment, parallel to the north side of Enclosure 1 suggests they could be of a similar date.

Enclosure 2

At some time after the cutting of the Enclosure 1 ditch and the construction of Structure 1, a second, much larger ditched enclosure (Enclosure 2; Fig 4) was established. Parts of the new ditch completely excised the western side of Enclosure 1.

Pl 9. Section through Enclosure 1 ditch F379, showing tripartite fills, looking west. Scale 30cm.

The observed lengths of ditch described the south and west sides of a probably quadrangular enclosure with sides at least 70m long on the former and 64m on the latter. There was a gap in the ditch on the western side, 3.5m wide. If this causeway was situated centrally, then the western side of the enclosure was approximately 77m long. No particular features defined the entrance, the northern side being a simple butt-end, the opposite side terminating in a curving return. The irregularity in the plan of the latter is noteworthy and possibly a sign of the recutting and repositioning of the entrance.

The ditch of Enclosure 2, (F11/F41/F302) varied in width and depth but was generally no greater than 2m wide and 1.5m deep (Fig 7). It was filled with grey brown clay silts

(10, 40, 301, 369 and 424) containing pottery, animal bone, Roman tile, charcoal and flints. In most places finds were relatively few in number but sections cut on the southern side of the enclosure, away from Structure 1, yielded greater quantities of occupation debris. The primary fill (369) of the enclosure ditch, where investigated on the south side, consisted of 0.30m of light coloured silty-clay containing daub, charcoal, animal bones, tile and flint. A significant quantity of pottery was recovered from this deposit, datable to the late third or early fourth century. However, the darker upper fill here (40) yielded by far the largest assemblage of pottery from the entire site, as well as a significant assemblage of coins, some of which were lost through the activity of metal detectorists; those recovered formed a series closing in AD 290. The dating of the pottery is broadly in keeping with that of the associated coinage in suggesting a very late third- or early fourth-century date for its deposition, and by implication, the final backfilling of the ditch. Similar occupation debris (42/43) was found as a thin layer over the natural on both sides of the ditch in this area and may have derived from dumping of domestic refuse. Whatever its source the occurrence outside the ditch suggests it had been deposited after the filling of the ditch or had been scattered by later disturbance; the condition of the deposits and the natural surface suggested disturbance from the trampling of animals.

The date for the infilling of the ditch and the deposition of the occupation debris is broadly similar to that indicated for the abandonment and final infilling of Structure 1, and suggests that any significant Roman occupation of the site had ceased by the end of the third century or shortly after,

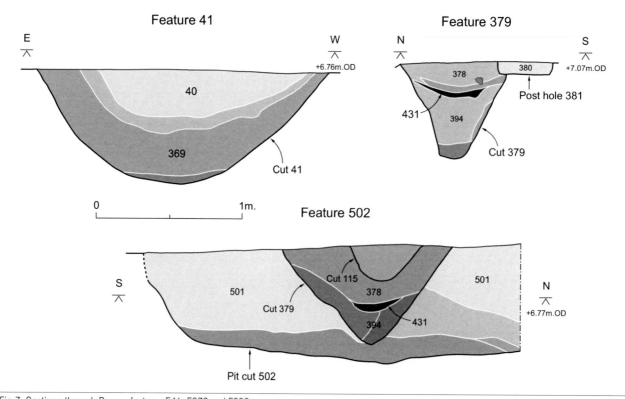

Fig 7. Sections through Roman features F41, F379 and F502.

particularly as there was no pottery of an exclusively fourth-century date. Although it would appear that the western ditch of Enclosure 2 cuts off or replaces the end of Enclosure 1, that the two enclosures were contemporaneous is indicated by the interdigitating fills at the junction of ditches F302 and F379, particularly the charcoal layer (442/431) derived from the firing of Structure 1 which also clearly extended into the semi-backfilled ditch of Enclosure 2.

Few features that can be definitely ascribed to the Roman period were found within Enclosure 2, apart from a possible cremation burial. This consisted of a small pit (F187), 1.03m long, 0.37m broad and 0.05m deep, with a rounded profile and burnt base and sides which lay about 20m to the east of Structure 1. It was filled with a grey silty-clay and brown silt (186) that produced a significant amount of calcined bone and one hobnail, besides charred plant remains including rye and barley grains, suggestive of an unurned cremation burial of Roman date. One other small and shallow feature (F482) on the western side of the enclosure and just north of Enclosure 1 also yielded a more significant, though still relatively small assemblage of Roman pottery.

Period 3: Anglo-Saxon

The Roman settlement was superseded by Anglo-Saxon occupation consisting of two or more structures, associated enclosures and pit complexes of possibly more than one phase (Fig 8). The dating evidence for these features is sparse and, although a relative chronology for the sequence of structures and enclosures to the east can be postulated or, in some cases, determined through stratigraphic relationships, it is impossible to be sure whether the buildings preceded the enclosures or vice-versa.

Enclosure 3

Roman Enclosure 2 was superseded by Enclosure 3 which went through several phases of enlargement and modification. The new enclosure occupied the eastern part of its predecessor, overlapping its eastern side at an angle of 45 degrees. Enclosure 3 was a polygonal area 38m wide by over 25m long and contained one structure (Structure 3) on a similar alignment (Figs 3 and 7). This strongly suggests that structure and enclosure were coeval. The south-eastern side of the enclosure was represented by ditch F326, a linear feature aligned north-east/south-west. The ditch extended beyond the site boundary to the north-east, and was traced 23m to the south-west, where it became wider before it terminated with a probable rounded end. Although mostly removed here by a later ditch (F99), the south-western terminus clearly cut the fills of ditch F41 of Roman Enclosure 2. Its width varied along its length, from a minimum of 0.7m to a maximum of 2.40m; this variation in width may be due to the wetness of the clay subsoil in this part of the site, which was of a different composition than elsewhere and specked with manganese, suggesting a waterlogged

environment (Courty et al 1989, 8, 185). One section was excavated, revealing straight, sloping sides curving sharply onto a narrow, flat base 0.69m deep (Fig 12). The fill (325) was a light orange-brown silty-clay with charcoal and daub inclusions, but otherwise sterile.

The north-western and south-eastern sides of the enclosure in this first phase were almost certainly represented by ditch F127 which was in three continuous but differently aligned lengths, totalling 34m. The northernmost section, about 12m long, was aligned approximately north-east/south-west, similar to the other side of the enclosure, which lay about 38m to the east. The ditch then curved abruptly to a near north–south alignment for a length of nearly 16m. It thereafter curved more gently to the east for another 6m where it terminated against a pit (F332) in an indeterminate relationship. The ditch may have originally extended further to the east however, but had been removed by truncation, since its dwindling width towards this terminal suggests that it was becoming more eroded. The orientation of this section, which is directly aligned on the southern terminus of ditch F326, may also suggest this, and that there was originally a much narrower entrance in this position.

Sections were excavated in two positions of the ditch; at its intersection with pit F604 and at the northern edge of the site; these revealed a shallow U-shaped profile of width between 0.30 and 0.80m, and edges sloping gradually onto a base 0.19m deep at maximum. The fill (126) was a grey-brown silty-clay with charcoal and daub inclusions, but mostly devoid of pottery, producing just one Anglo-Saxon and a few Roman sherds.

Structure 3 and associated features

Structure 3 was situated in the western half of Enclosure 3, and was the best preserved and most completely exposed of the post-Roman buildings (Fig 9). Although there was little directly associated dating evidence, it was clear from its form and its relation to other presumed post-Roman features that it also belonged to this later phase of occupation.

The structure, almost entirely delineated by post-settings, was approximately rectangular with long axis set north-east/south-west (about 45 degrees out of alignment with the main Roman enclosure), and although its width was fully exposed, its north-eastern limit or side was not located and a relatively modern ditch (F99) may have removed some elements of its south-western end. Nonetheless, the structure's extent can be fairly accurately inferred.

The building was probably about 14m long and about 6m wide, its outer wall lines defined by single, or sometimes double post-settings, set varying distances apart, although towards the north-eastern end of the building in particular the post-holes were often very close together. The shallowness of many post-holes, some of large dimensions, suggests considerable horizontal truncation of the structural remains. The area of the extreme north-eastern end of the building was unavailable due to the line of the high-voltage cable while the south-western end had possibly also been truncated. In

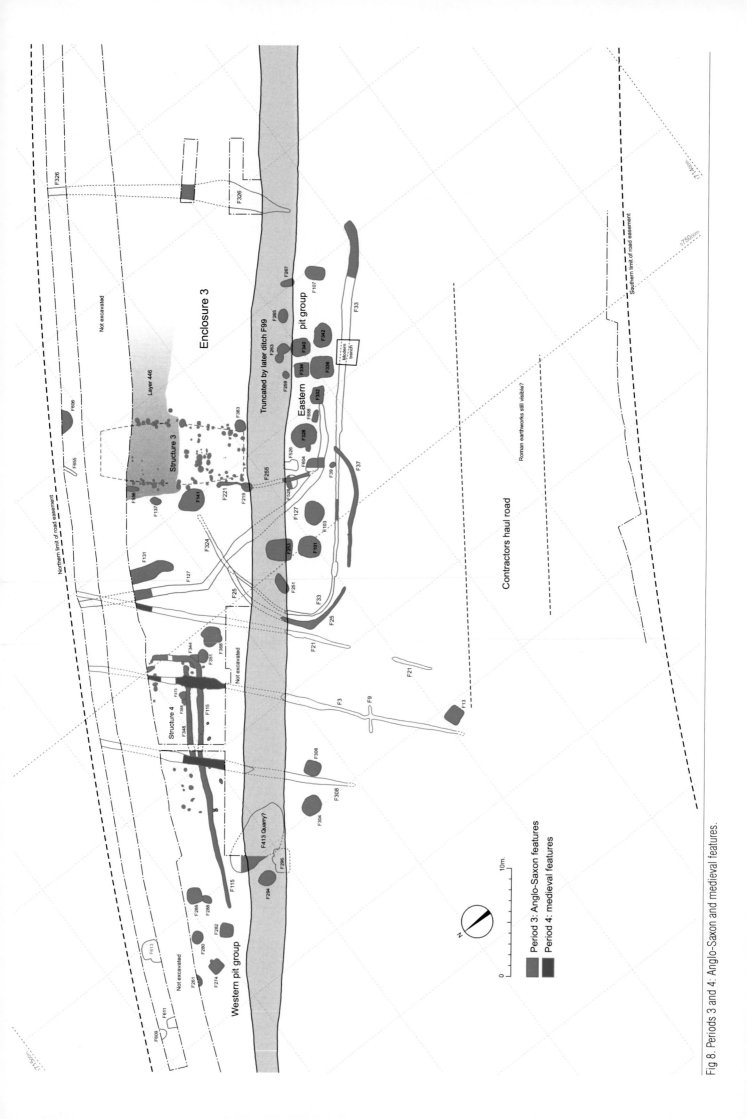

F326

Northern limit of road easement

F606

Not excavated

F655

Enclosure 3

Layer 446

Structure 3

F383

Truncated by later ditch F99

F326

F267

F265

F263

Eastern pit group

F107

F33

F259

F342

F340

F336

Modern trench

F334

F332

F686

F328

F526

F526

F526

F604

F39

F37

F255

F221

F219

F141

F356

F137

F131

F127

F324

F127

F253

F101

F103

F261

F33

F25

F25

F25

F21

F21

Contractors haul road

Roman earthworks still visible?

Southern limit of road easement

17140mm

5750mm

F13

F3

F9

F344

F351

F368

Structure 4

F373

F386

F115

F348

Not excavated

F115

F306

F308

F413 Quarry?

F304

F296

F294

F115

F286

F288

F282

Western pit group

F281

F280

F274

Not excavated

F613

F611

F609

17150mm

N

0   10m.

Period 3: Anglo-Saxon features

Period 4: medieval features

Fig 8. Periods 3 and 4: Anglo-Saxon and medieval features.

this latter respect however, the position of post-holes F494 and F209/401 in relation to the structure's longitudinal axis, suggest that these had formed part of an end wall. The position of a pit, (F219), also suggested that this lay immediately beyond the south-western corner and formed part of the series of cess-pits in the area to the south. The same may hold true for pit F383 adjacent to the south-eastern corner, although this was of significantly different form to most of the other pits and it could potentially be of a slightly later date.

Prominent clusters of large posts on either side, 7m from the south-western end of the structure, presumably marked opposing doorways which, if placed centrally in each side, as in many comparable structures, would imply an overall length of approximately 14m.

The surviving post-holes did not form a regular or rectangular pattern as in many contemporary buildings, but those around the perimeter suggest a building with slightly bowed sides or tapering towards the surviving end. The clusters of major post-holes flanking the presumed doorways (F530, F532, F534, F600 and F602 on the west and F145, F590, F592, F594, F596 and F598 on the east) may have supported not only the door-frames but also carried major structural timbers, perhaps a cruck-frame to support the roof in the centre of the building. The oval outline of many post-holes may suggest their recutting while elsewhere along the perimeter the noticeable pairing of timbers suggests a form of wall construction in which horizontal wall planks were clasped between pairs of uprights (James *et al* 1984, 194–5, fig 9).

Other sockets in the south-western end of the interior appear to mark subdivisions or the outline of a room at that end. Slighter post-holes F179, F181, F185, F189 and F522 marked an internal division 2m from the centre line of the cross passage and 4.5m from the end of the building. Two substantial sockets F163/486 and F175 near the centreline and close to this cross wall (and perhaps F177 and F426 further south) may have served as supports for the ridge line but these were not part of a regular series along the centreline and the main roof structure must have been predominantly supported by the exterior posts. These central post-settings could conceivably be later additions however, placed during a period of repair or as additional support. The central and north-eastern end of the structure revealed no features other than six minor stake-holes, although the disposition of three of these (F560, F562 and F566) is again suggestive of a mostly eradicated internal partition.

No trace of interior surfaces survived but any floor covering had probably rested on the natural surface. This is suggested, in particular, in the north-eastern half of the structure which was at a slightly deeper level and marked by a slight scarp, approximately 0.10m deep, running between the post-holes on the south side of the opposing doorways. This drop in level may have been caused by wear or erosion

Pl 10. Structure 3, looking south-west. Scale 2m.

to the soft clay subsoil, although it may have been deliberate since the post-holes in this north-eastern area were generally slightly deeper than those to the south. In any event, it suggests that the north-eastern part of the building had a markedly different function to the south-western end. The lower level was filled with a darker soil (446) containing charcoal and daub, similar to that filling many of the post-holes. This soil extended outside the wall to the east so was not directly the result of the occupation of the interior; the amount of burnt debris suggests that at least one phase of the building was destroyed by fire.

There was little dating evidence from the structural remains, although thirteen of the post-hole fills each yielded one, or sometimes two, small Roman sherds. These were contemporary with the main phase of Roman occupation and are considered to be residual.

Immediately adjacent to the structure on the north-west were three short lengths of discontinuous gully, aligned approximately north-east/south-west; F556 to the north of the main excavated area, and F221 and F255 to the south. A similar gully, F655, exposed in the slit trench to the north-east may be part of the same system, but was on a slightly more east-westerly alignment. All were of similar width and depth where investigated. F255, the most fully excavated was 0.25m wide, and 0.18 to 0.4m deep, with a steep-sided profile curving to a flat base (Fig 12).[4] The fill (254), was a dark grey-brown silty-clay, which contained very frequent pieces of crushed mussel shell in its upper part. Other inclusions included charcoal and daub and flint pebbles and a few sherds of Roman pottery.

There are a number of possible interpretations for these gullies, but because of their position, they were obviously directly associated with Structure 3, and perhaps the most likely is that they were for drainage around the structure. Unfortunately, the relationship between F255 and enclosure ditch F127 remained indeterminate; however, the relationship of gully F255 and pit F528, which it was recorded as cutting, would suggest the gully was the later

---

4   The gully was generally shallow, but became much deeper where it cut across an underlying pit F528 (Fig 12), which suggests that the pit had only recently been backfilled and the ground was still uncompacted.

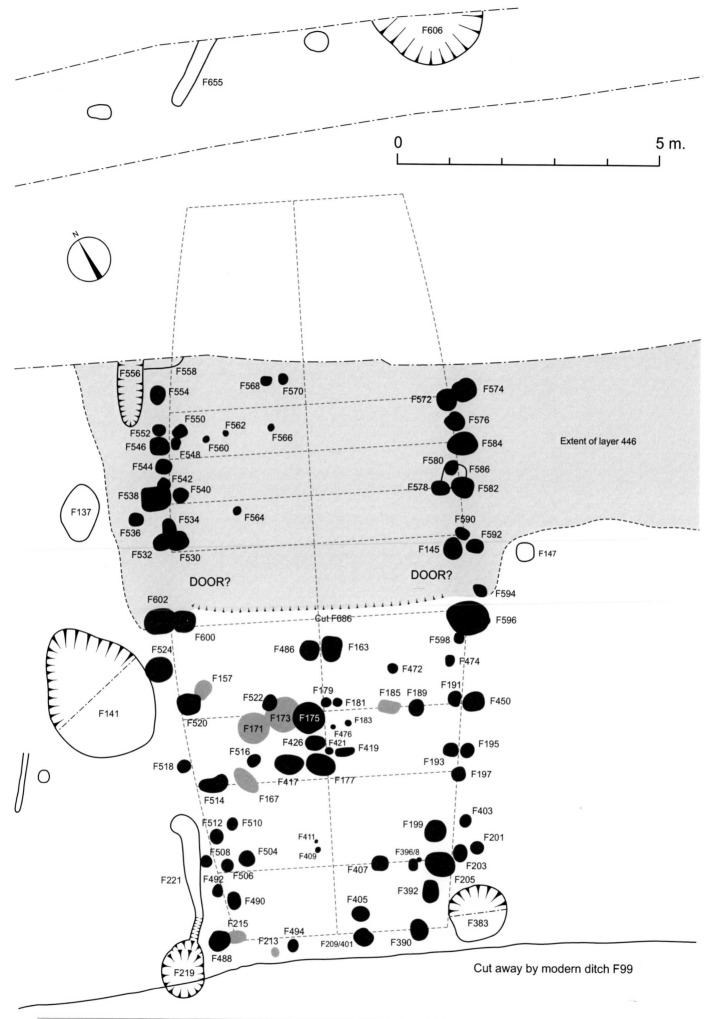

Fig 9. Plan of Structure 3.

feature and was perhaps draining into a depression left by the ditch. However, topographical factors strongly suggest that the structure and pits were contemporary, so it may be that the shallow gully was a much later recut of an earlier drain, inserted whilst the building was still standing.

Modifications to Enclosure 3

The enclosure around the building was subsequently modified or enlarged with the insertion of ditch F33, which cut ditch F127 of the primary enclosure.[5] To the south the main part of this ditch was aligned north-west/south-east and was about 34m long, extending to, and just beyond the backfilled Roman ditch of Enclosure 2, which it cut. At this end, which was in line with a projected continuation of ditch F326 forming the eastern arm of the enclosure, the cut just curved to the east, and ended in a squared off terminal; these terminals formed an entrance into the enclosure about 5m wide. To the west, the cut curved to the north and north-east where it was removed by a modern ditch (F99). North of here the ditch continued, aligned near east–west, for about 7m. The end of the ditch was not well defined and appeared to fade away rather than terminate, possibly due to truncation. If its alignment continued however, it would have extended to just south of the proposed doorway of Structure 3.

The cut was of varying width, but widest at the south-eastern terminal, where it measured about 1m. Generally however the cut was less than 0.5m wide. A 5m length of F33 was excavated at its south-eastern terminal and a shorter slot 20m to the north-west. The short length of the cut north of F99 was not excavated. The profile was generally flat based with a steeper edge to the north and a slight step on the southern side, possibly the result of recutting. The profile became more U-shaped towards the south-eastern terminal where the step disappeared. It was about 0.30m deep at the south-eastern end. The fill (32) was a mid to dark grey to grey brown silty-clay with rare charcoal inclusions, but otherwise sterile apart from a quantity of Roman sherds, probably derived from the underlying Roman ditch F41.

The position of the terminals of both ditches F33 and the probably contemporaneous F326, over the line of the earlier Roman ditch of Enclosure 2, may indicate that, although mostly backfilled, it was still visible as a residual depression. Certain other topological factors also suggest this may have been the case, although the alignment of the Roman enclosure system does not appear to have influenced the alignment of the post-Roman enclosure. It may be noted however, that the central length of ditch F127 is on a very similar alignment to the western side of Roman Enclosure 2, although this may be coincidence.

A subsequent more minor modification, represented by ditches F25 and F37, merely redefined the protruding western corner of the enclosure delineated by F33. F25 was crescent-shaped in plan with two curved terminals at its eastern and southern ends, and was about 15m long altogether. Ditch F25 was c 0.50m wide at maximum, but was not excavated, although its later relationship to ditch F33 was clear in plan. Its fill (24) was a very dark grey silty-clay. The course of this ditch segment was continued after a short gap, further to the east by ditch F37. This section was aligned north-west/south-east, 11m long and c 0.30m wide, but it curved slightly to the east at its eastern end where it was seen to cut F33. The cut terminated to the east and west with rounded butt-ends. A 1m long slot was excavated through the feature, which revealed a shallow cut of 0.07m maximum depth, with sloping edges and an uneven base. The fill (36) was a mid dark grey brown, mottled brown silty-clay, which yielded little artefactual evidence.

In both these later phases the curving outline of the corner, returning on the east towards the entrance on the north-west side of Structure 3, suggested that the gullies defined the area occupied by the pit complex and channelled traffic from the south towards this entrance of the building. The contents of the gullies do not provide evidence for their date or relationship to the use of the building, since only residual Roman pottery was recovered, but it seems extremely likely that they all relate to its period of use.

Pits and other features within the enclosure

A group of over twenty pits was found immediately to the south-west of Structure 3, all within the area defined by the modified Enclosure 3 and clearly respecting the line of ditch F33 in particular. Little conclusive dating evidence was recovered from most of these features, but their contemporaneity with the structure and associated enclosure is therefore clear on topographic grounds. About 50 per cent of the features were half excavated, and these are described below. A further five pits or other features within the enclosed area are also probably contemporary. The fills often suggested an organic fill consistent with their use as cess-pits. In some cases samples were taken to test this hypothesis and these are described below (*see* p 67).

Pit F101 at the north-western end of the group consisted of an approximately circular cut of 2m diameter, 1.30m deep with a steep-sided and flat-based profile (Fig 11). The fill (100) consisted of eight deposits some of which appeared to be slumped. These were mostly brown and green-brown silty-clays with some layers of redeposited brickearth, particularly at the base. The inclusions were of varying concentrations of charcoal, daub (particularly in the upper fills) and pebbles, but the fills were otherwise sterile. The edges of the feature were stained green, and this, its profile and the nature of the fills suggest that it had been used as a cess-pit.

Pit F103 immediately south-east of F101 was oval in plan, measuring 1.80m by 2.22m, and was 1.29m deep (Fig 11). Its profile was steep-sided, curving into a rounded base.

---

5.   This relationship was more obvious in plan than section due to the shallowness of the ditches at this point.

Six fills were given one number (102). They consisted of grey-brown and grey-green silty-clays layered alternately with redeposited brickearth, which was the main basal layer. Inclusions included varying concentrations of daub, carbon and gravel. Animal bone, Roman pottery and tile were also present but in very small quantities. Some of the fills appeared to have a high organic content. The profile of the feature, the clear slumping of its fills and also the slightly organic nature of some fills, were characteristic of it being a cess-pit.

Pit F107, the south-easternmost of the group was subrectangular, measuring 1.85 by 1.2m. It was 1.15m deep, with steeply sloped sides and a flat base. The fill (106) consisted of three separate deposits slumping towards the centre of the feature. The primary level was of dark brown silty-clay with charcoal and stone inclusions, 0.12m thick, which was overlain by a 0.60m thick deposit of mid to light brown silty-clay with charcoal inclusions. The uppermost fill, of depth 0.45m, was not described. Green staining on the sides of the pit, its profile, and the slumping were characteristic of a cess-pit.

Pit F251 was an approximately oval cut, truncated from above by modern ditch F99 at the extreme north-western end of the group. Its dimensions following truncation were 2m by 1m; depth would have been in excess of 0.95m while the profile was of a U-shape with fairly steep sides. The fill (250) was a grey-brown silty-clay with charcoal and stone inclusions. Very small quantities of animal bone and Roman pot were also recovered.

Pit F253, adjacent to F251 was a subrectangular cut, the northern part of which had been removed by later ditch F99. The dimensions following truncation were 2.65m by 2 m; to the south it survived to a depth of 1.80m with steep sides and a flat base, though there was a slight step about 1m down. The deposits within the cut were collectively numbered (252). These comprised at least nine slumped layers of silty-clays with varying concentrations of charcoal inclusions and were of varying colour, brown at the top with much gravel incorporated, and grey towards the base. The lower fills had a greater organic content. Animal bone, Roman pottery and some tile were also recovered. The pit profile, its fills and slumping were characteristic of a cess-pit.

Pit F265 was an oval-shaped cut, measuring 1.36 by 1m which was also truncated from above by modern ditch F99; it survived to a depth of only 0.45m but would originally have been in excess of 0.8m deep. The portion remaining possessed vertical sides curving sharply to a flat base. The fill (264) was a mid dark grey-olive grey silty-clay, with charcoal, tile, two small sherds of Roman pottery, daub, and also flint/pebble inclusions. Greenish staining of the cut edges was characteristic of a cess-pit.

Pit F267 was a long oval cut, measuring 1.40m by 0.75m. Truncated from above by ditch F99, its original depth would have been about 0.60m, but its remaining U-shaped profile survived to only 0.35m. Its fill (266) was a mid olive grey-greenish grey silty, slightly sandy, clay. The inclusions were of Roman pottery, charcoal, and flint pebbles. There was a

layer, about 0.10m deep of redeposited natural in the base of the cut, but no obvious evidence that it was a cess-pit.

A subrectangular cut F336, measured 1.9m by 2.2m and was excavated to a depth of 1.35m but not bottomed. Its edges were steep or near vertical. The fill (335) consisted of six slumped deposits, mostly brown silty-clay layered with redeposited brickearth. The inclusions were of varying quantities of flint, stone and charcoal. Some animal bone, Roman pottery and tile were also present as well as a fibre processing spike of probable Anglo-Saxon date (see p 23). The profile of the pit and the slumping of the layers suggest that it had been used as a cess-pit.

Pit F340 was subrectangular to oval in plan, measuring 1.92 by 1.65m and in excess of 1.4m deep (Fig 12). Its shape became more rectangular with depth while the edges sloped steeply, stepping inwards slightly at about half the excavated depth. The pit was not bottomed for safety reasons, but probing showed that it continued for at least another metre in depth, ie the total depth was in excess of 2.40m. The edges of the cut were stained bright yellow/green. The fill (339) consisted of seven different deposits. The lower layers were grey, grey-brown or green-grey silty-clays with varying proportions of charcoal and grit inclusions. They slumped towards the centre of the pit and appeared to become more gritty and organic with depth. A sample (7) taken from the lower fill of this feature did not provide any positive evidence for the presence of cess. Yellow powdery concretions recovered may be the poorly preserved remains of cess, although they did not look like typical faecal concretions such as were noted in samples 8 and 8a from the fills of F344. The uppermost fill consisted of a thick layer of redeposited brickearth, interpreted as a possible capping layer. Relatively large amounts of animal bone, Iron Age and Roman pottery, tile and some larger pieces of burnt clay were recovered.

Pit F528 consisted of an oval cut, measuring 1.3 by 1.1m (Fig 12). Its uppermost fills appear to have been cut by linear feature F255, associated with Structure 3. The sides sloped steeply or vertically onto a flat base, 0.80m deep. The fill (527) was composed of eight slumped deposits. The primary fill was an orange-brown redeposited brickearth, which was present mainly along the edges of the cut. The later fills consisted in the main of grey and green-grey silty-clays with varying concentrations of carbon, flint flakes, daub, sea shell, animal bone and Roman pot inclusions. A loomweight fragment (p 21) and a set of Anglo-Saxon tweezers (pp 18–20) of seventh- or eighth-century date were also recovered. The deposits appeared to become more organic with depth. The profile of the cut, the slumping, and also the organic content of the fills were characteristic of a cess-pit.

Finally, pit F604 was an oval to subrectangular cut, measuring approximately 1.5 by 1.2m (Fig 12). In profile the sides sloped steeply or vertically onto a flat base, 1.43m deep. The edges of the lower half of the pit were stained green. The six fills were collectively numbered (603). The lower fills consisted of a cess-like level, and a basal deposit with a higher gravel content. The later fills consisted of slumped layers of grey-brown and green silty-clays with varying concentrations of charcoal, daub and gravel inclusions. There was also a layer of redeposited brickearth. The profile of the pit, the staining of the edges, slumping of the layers and apparent cess content of the fills, implies that it had been used as a cess-pit. The feature also yielded the only sherds of Anglo-Saxon pottery of the entire group, including two of Ipswich ware (*see* p 43). The pit had an undetermined relationship with ditch F127 of Enclosure 3, but the arrangement of the pit group must indicate that the pit was the later feature.[6]

Pits F526, F688, F259, F334, F332 and F263 remained unexamined due to time constraints, but there is no reason to suppose that they were much different to those described above.[7]

A few other features may also be contemporary. A circular cut 0.55m in diameter (F39) was situated just south of the pit group, immediately adjacent to ditch F33. It was not excavated. A much larger feature (F141, Fig 11) was located immediately to the west of Structure 3, just south of its presumed central doorway. It was an approximately oval cut measuring 2.7 by 2.1m. In profile, the sides were undercut, leading to a flat base of 1.07m maximum depth. The fill (140) consisted of four distinct deposits. The primary fill was of redeposited brickearth, existing to a maximum depth of 0.20m and sealed by a 0.64m deep level of a mid brown silty-clay. Above this was a dark grey silty-clay, 0.34m deep. The uppermost level was a mid brown silty-clay, 0.42m deep, with common charcoal and daub inclusions. A few sherds of Roman pottery were recovered. Charred cereal grains and seeds were common in Sample 1 taken from the lower fill of this feature (*see* p 67). Small fragments of mammal bone, some of which had been burnt, and traces of mussel shell were also present. There was no indication of cess having been present, but the pit clearly contained several distinct deposits and only one of these was sampled. Slightly to the north-east of this pit, a smaller unexcavated feature (F137), may also relate to this phase, being immediately adjacent to Structure 3.

Some way north-east of Structure 3 and at the extreme northern limit of the site was a possible pit F606, which was only partially exposed and excavated. The feature was probably oval in plan, extending 2.30m along, and 1m from, the trench edge. The sides were steep, more so on the eastern edge, and the base was in excess of 0.8m deep (the feature was not bottomed). The fill (605), was a grey-brown silty-clay with charcoal and daub, and stone inclusions, from which a few sherds of Roman pottery were recovered.

Two features were found directly beside the presumed south-western corners of Structure 3, both differing in form but too large to possibly represent components of the building. Pit F219 on the south-west corner was a circular cut of 0.85m diameter (Fig 11). Its sides were vertical, meeting

a flat base 1.11m deep. The uppermost south edge of the pit had been partially truncated by ditch F99. The pit bore an undetermined relationship with gully F221, bordering the edge of Structure 3 to the north-east. The fill (218) was a mid grey-brown silty-clay, with an increasing light grey-green silt content towards the base. Inclusions were of carbon flecks and daub, and twenty-five sherds of Roman pottery and tile pieces were also recovered. A significant quantity of sheep bone, mostly from an articulated skeleton of a very young animal, was also found. The sides of the pit were stained a greenish grey hue. Its profile, fill and the stained edges were characteristic of a cess-pit, but as with pit F340 to the south a sample (Sample 3, context 218, F219, p 67) did not provide definite evidence for the presence of cess, although similar yellow concretions to those seen in Sample 7 (context 399, F340, p 66) were noted. Pit F383 was adjacent to the south-east corner of the building. It was oval to subrectangular in plan, measuring 1.0 by 1.1m. In profile the sides sloped near vertically, curving onto a flat base, 0.42m deep. The primary fill (385), was a 0.17m thick mixed layer of light-grey and orange-brown silty-clay. This was sealed by a 0.6m deep layer (384), a mixture of dark grey and light-brown silty-clay with charcoal and daub inclusions. The uppermost fill (382) was 0.30m deep, and consisted of a grey-brown silty-clay with carbon and gravel inclusions from which an Anglo-Saxon iron pin was recovered (*see* p 48). All the fills yielded a small quantity of Roman sherds.

One other feature (F131), partially exposed to the north of the site may be contemporary with the enclosure because of its alignment, but it was very shallow and no finds were recovered even though it was fully excavated.

Pits F141 and F606 north-east of the main group of features could conceivably be Roman in date, although they contained considerable quantities of daub, similar to those pits that can be confidently ascribed to this phase. Pits F219 and F383 although slightly apart from the main group are almost certainly of the Anglo-Saxon period due to their spatial relationship to Structure 3 and the finds from F383. Of interest here is pit F219, which contained the articulated bones of a young sheep. This is comparable to a contemporary pit of possibly similar function from one of the Channel Tunnel excavations near Folkestone which contained a neonatal sheep skeleton (Bendrey 2002).

Although the main group of pits south-west of Structure 3 were of similar size, their depth was more variable, but most of those examined possessed similar characteristics. They were normally subrectangular or oval in plan, with vertical-sided and flat-based profiles. The sequence of backfills, often sterile artefactually, also demonstrated similarities; there was heavy greenish staining of the edges of the cut, and a high organic content to some of the deposits. These factors suggest that the features were used as cess-pits,

---

6. There is some confusion in the site records about the relationship between ditch F127 and pit F604. It is suggested that this occurred due to the cutting of what is likely to have been a later feature (F255) at this exact location (*see* p 17).

7. F263 has here been allocated to two intercutting features, one of which was double numbered (268) on site.

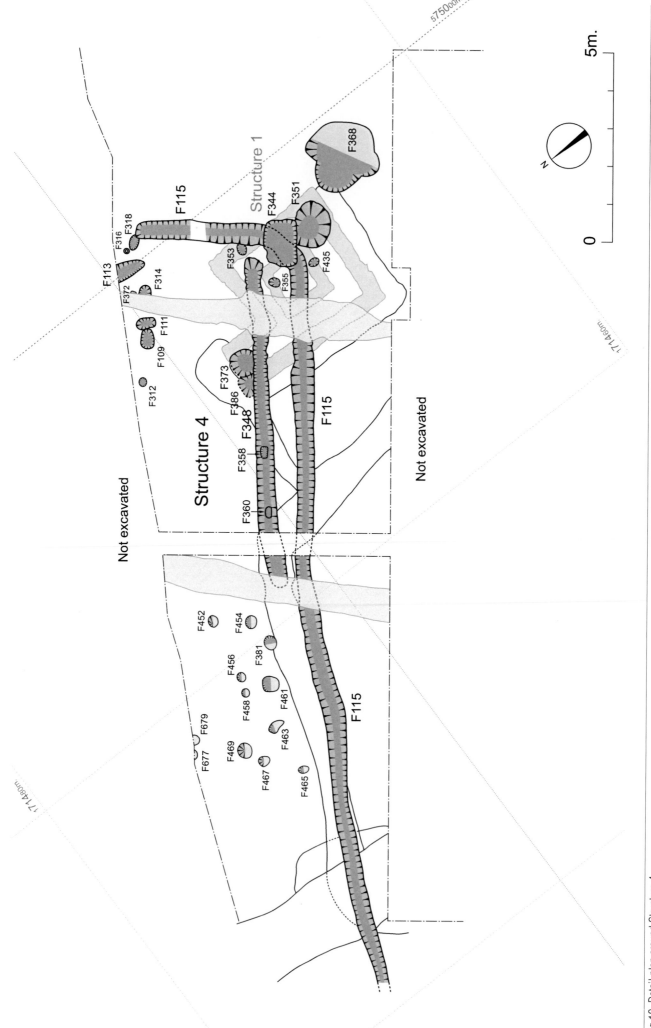

Fig 10. Detail plan around Structure 4.

although this was not directly confirmed by environmental analysis. It remains possible therefore that at least some of them may have possessed a different function, although there was obviously a heavy organic content. This is further discussed below.

Although only a few of the pits can be dated from their content, it seems likely that all of this group are related to Structure 3. Their formality in layout and the alignment and disposition of the features, is clearly based on the boundaries represented by the Enclosure 3 ditches, particularly F33. In addition, apart from one instance (F263 and F268), none of the features intercut; they were obviously laid out not to do so, with many closely juxtaposed. This is very unlikely to have happened by chance, and is not only suggestive of their primary function, the removal of human or other organic waste but further indicates that all must have been cut, used and probably backfilled as part of the same and continuous occupation phase. Indeed, the layout (particularly the closely arranged F334 and F336) might even suggest that most of the pits were open and functioning at the same time, or if not, the position of those backfilled must have been remembered, or was perhaps still clear on the ground through residual slumping. Many of these features contained upper fills very similar to that of the possible destruction layer (F446) of Structure 3, also suggestive (if nothing more) of contemporaneity.

In detail, the backfill sequence varied considerably, although the individual components were often alike from pit to pit. Basal layers were often redeposited brickearth, usually immediately superseded by organic or degraded organic material. The basal levels were probably produced by erosion to the edges of the cuts, which suggests that the pits were left open for some time.

The presumed cess or organic-like levels were nearly always sealed by deposits of gravel and clay, almost certainly thrown into the pits to cover the offensive deposits at the base. In one case, F604, a similar gravel deposit over the presumed base of the cut may intimate that the bottom of this feature was not actually reached. Secondary organic deposits sometimes overlay the gravel (eg F103), but usually it was sealed by further layers of redeposited brickearth or other material. Some of these may represent rubbish disposal (mostly organic), but the brickearth deposits more probably represent natural erosion and suggest a hiatus in backfilling. The upper levels of surviving fill very often contained a high proportion of burnt clay or charcoal, or at least discrete lenses of this material. It is tempting to relate these deposits to the possible destruction of Structure 3, or other buildings in the vicinity, some debris having been dumped into the hollows formed from the settling of their contents.

Some truncation of the pits is indicated by the internal morphology of their fills and tiplines, but it is not really possible to determine the depth of this truncation. Tip lines within F528 suggest that as much as 0.40m may have been lost.

Many of the pits contained some residual Roman material, but this is not unusual. Only one of the features

(F604) yielded Anglo-Saxon pottery, five eighth- or ninth-century sherds, including two of Ipswich ware (*see* p 43). Another of the group (F528) also contained Anglo-Saxon material, including loomweight fragments and a set of tweezers, although the latter may be earlier than the ceramics, perhaps seventh century AD. The little dating evidence therefore indicates an Anglo-Saxon date for the pit group, and by extension, the enclosure and its associated structure. This is likely to be middle Anglo-Saxon, with the emphasis on the period *c* AD 775–850, although there is some evidence for slightly earlier activity.

Possible contemporary structures, pits and other features outside the enclosure to the west of the site

Two groups of pits that almost certainly post-date the Roman occupation of the site were found to the west of Enclosure 3. Although the dating evidence for these features was similarly sparse, stratigraphic relationships with the Roman features clearly indicate a post-Roman provenance for most. The earliest of these pits (F373, F386 and F435) were cut by elements of Structure 4, so clearly pre-date that structure and may therefore relate to the occupation of Structure 3 to the east. The recovered artefacts, such as they are, suggest that the pits were roughly contemporary with Structure 3 and its associated enclosure and pits; they may therefore relate entirely with this phase of occupation. However, the largest group of pits on the western fringes of the site exhibit certain patterns of layout, that show no relation to the Structure 3 or its enclosure and it seems likely that they relate to the more proximate Structure 4.

The central pit group (Fig 10)

The earliest features of this group were two intercutting small pits or post-pits (F373 and F386) that intruded into the deposits and masonry of Structure 1 at its extreme north end. Their precise function is unclear. F373 was centrally cut within the flue of Structure 1 and just clipped the side walls but the earlier F386, more than half truncated the northern extremity of the western wall as well as cutting the latest fill of side drain F430. Both features predated Structure 4 since they were cut by its southern wall slot F348.

Pit F386 was a subrectangular cut, measuring 0.30 by 0.25m. It was cut on its eastern edge by feature F373, and itself cut into the western flue wall F92 of the underlying Structure 1. In profile it had sides sloping gradually onto an almost flat base, 0.32m deep. The fill (387) was a mid grey-brown silty-clay with chalk, angular flint, carbon, some Roman tile and daub inclusions, but no pottery or other dating evidence was recovered although it was fully excavated.

Pit F373 was approximately square, measuring 0.72 by 0.74m. The corners and sides were quite rounded although F348 had cut the southern edge. In profile the sides sloped steeply onto a rounded base 0.43m deep. The fill (95) was a dark grey-brown silty-clay with chalk, considerable Roman tile and brick, flint and daub inclusions. Residual Roman pottery (two sherds) was also present. The high chalk and tile content were probably derived from its cutting of the Structure 1 flue, which suggests that the feature may have been a post-pit, with the excavated masonry re-used as packing, but there was no sign of a post ghost.

Just to the south-east of these, a further three juxtaposed pits (F344, F351 and F368) also cut into the deposits and fabric relating to the Roman Structure 1, here about 5m to the west of Enclosure 3. Of these, F344 and the earlier F351 were situated within the south-east corner of Structure 1 and were fully excavated. Both cut into the inner and outer walls of the building, and probably pre-dated Structure 4. Feature F368 was situated immediately outside the south-east corner of Structure 1, where it just clipped the backfill of the southern drain F445. This may have consisted of two intercutting pits, though the fills were indistinguishable.

Pit F351 was an oval cut, measuring 1.20 by 1m and 0.48m deep with a steep-sided and flat-based profile. The fill (350) was a mid dark brown, loose, silty-clay with chalk, charcoal and stone inclusions. Considerable quantities of Roman tile and brick may have originated from Structure 1, particularly the tile corner pad at the base of wall F83, which the pit had partially removed. Four sherds of Roman pottery were also probably residual.

Pit F344, which cut the northern edge of F351, consisted of a subrectangular cut measuring 1.3m by 0.90m, with a steep- to vertical-sided profile, curving onto a slightly concave base 0.82m deep. The lower fill (349) with a depth of 0.06m consisted of sterile light orange-yellow, loose, silty-clay with chalk flecks. Above this, the bulk of the feature was filled with mid grey-brown silty-clay containing variable amounts of redeposited brickearth or burnt clay (343). Other inclusions were of chalk, charcoal, daub, flint, animal bone, and some slag and Roman tile. Of more significance were pottery sherds of which the latest were of mid Anglo-Saxon date, c AD 700–850 (p 43). There were some possible traces of cess in this deposit. A sample from near the base of the pit (Sample 8a; p 67) yielded the mineralised remains of faeces and fragmentary fish bones that are commonly found in cess deposits; a sample from the upper fill (Sample 8) also indicated the presence of cess. Both samples contained small quantities of flake hammerscale, suggesting that some limited metalworking was occurring.

To the immediate south of these intercutting pits was F368, an amorphous shaped cut, appearing on excavation to be two features with identical fills (it possibly represented two oval/subrectangular cuts partially overlying one another). Its maximum dimensions were 2 by 2m with a depth of 0.43m. The profile was irregular and stepped (also suggesting the two cuts), whilst the seemingly uniform fill (367) was a

mixture of grey and pale brown silty-clays with carbon, daub and gravel inclusions. Some animal bone and Roman tile was also present. Twelve late Iron Age and Roman pottery sherds were also recovered, probably all residual. The feature just cut the upper fill (F443) of Structure 1 drain F445.

These features obviously post-date Structure 1, which indicates the likelihood of them all being post-Roman. Pit F344 contained the most significant dating evidence, a number of eighth- or ninth-century sherds. This would appear to be a cess-pit, but the function of the others is not so certain. Why these pits cut into the Roman structure is not clear. Both F344 and F351 are centred on the space between the inner and outer walls, but have still removed much fabric from the earlier structure. Both pits could have been quite easily dug elsewhere.

Structure 4 and associated features

Structure 4 was situated outside of Enclosure 3, c 7m to the west of ditch F127 (Fig 10). Its main component was a linear slot F348, aligned near north-west/south-east, and c 8.5–9m long, which was nearly all excavated. Its north-western terminus had been removed by a later field ditch F308.[8] The feature cut the uppermost fill of Enclosure 1 ditch F379 at this end. The south-eastern end was approximately squared, and cut through the masonry and rubble infill of, as well as terminating within, Roman Structure 1. It also cut drains F90 and F430, around the structure as well as two earlier pits (F373 and F386) about 3m from its end. The width of F348 varied between 0.40 and 0.50 m. Its profile was steep-sided, curving onto a flat base, with a maximum depth of 0.25m. The fill (347) was a mid dark grey silty-clay with common charcoal and daub inclusions rather less tile or brick fragments and animal bone. The most significant dating evidence however was five mid Anglo-Saxon sherds; an Anglo-Saxon bone pin (p 48), almost certainly misattributed to, or intrusive within Roman ditch F90, may also have derived from this feature, or perhaps the adjacent and related feature F115.

Two post-holes (F358 and F360), apparently sealed by (347), were found in the base of the cut, aligned on and with, its axis. These were 1.6m apart from centre to centre. F358 was rectangular in plan, 0.40m long (aligned with the axis of F348) and 0.22m wide. The sides were near vertical, rounding onto a U-shaped base of 0.15m maximum depth. The fill (357) comprised a lower layer of mid light orange-grey silty-clay with flint and carbon inclusions and an upper layer of mid dark grey silty-clay with flint, daub and carbon inclusions. A fragment of a middle Anglo-Saxon iron pin was also retrieved (p 48). Feature F360 was similarly rectangular and arranged, measuring 0.30 by 0.18m with an identical profile, depth and fill. No finds were recovered from this feature.

---

8. One peculiar feature of F348 that requires explanation is this western end, which was planned as slightly off-line to the south. This may be due to the exact juxtaposition of its northern edge with the underlying Roman ditch which made location of the edges of the later feature particularly difficult. Alternatively, but less likely considering the time difference between the two features, is residual slumping of the Roman ditch backfill, which may have moved this entire end of F348 southwards.

Pl 11. View of site looking east, showing Structure 3 under excavation.

The nature of F348 and the obviously associated post-holes in its base clearly suggest that it was a structural element, a slot representing the wall line of a building. Although no other post settings were located at the base of this slot, if the spacing between the two post-holes is extrapolated to both east and west, then postulated posts at these intervals exactly fit into the extent of F348. The presence of the post-holes at the base of the slot suggest that it was a trench excavated to take posts directly rather than for a ground beam, but it is not clear why only two of the postulated post-settings left a trace. They possibly bore more structural weight, or were deliberately set deeper into the ground.

No other structural elements can be positively attributed to Structure 4, although there were numerous post-holes in the vicinity. However, the line of the slot is extended to the west by a row of three further post-holes (F381, F461 and F463); these were of a smaller (although regular) spacing than those post-holes within the slot, and this spacing matched the distance of the row from the slot, which is highly suggestive of a structural relationship. The post-holes were of similar size and depth, approximately subrectangular, about 0.45 by 0.30m in extent, with steep-sided and flat-based profiles no more than 0.12m deep. Their fills were sterile, but F381 cut the backfilled ditch (F379) of Roman Enclosure 1, suggesting that it was of post-Roman date (Fig 10).

Few other post-holes in this area can be obviously associated with slot F348 although seven closely spaced post-settings about 3m to the north-east (F312, F109, F111, F314, F372, F316 and F318) do form a roughly parallel line, and another minimally examined cut F113, on the edge of the excavated area could conceivably represent a similar slot at right angles. Four other post-holes, F469, F677 and

F679 just to the north-west and F353 to the south-east could also conceivably relate to the structure, perhaps representing elements of its end walls. It seems likely however, that much of the structure has been lost, or was within the unexcavated area to the north (such as a parallel slot representing a northern wall line) and these factors preclude any definitive reconstruction of its form, although this, and its extent can be reasonably inferred.

Immediately adjacent to Structure 4, was ditch F115 which extended around the eastern and southern sides of the building in an 'L' shape. To the south-west, the ditch was about 0.9m away from the beam-slot F348, but to the south-east was less than 0.5m distant from its south-eastern terminal. The main length of the ditch was aligned north-west/south-east, exactly parallel to F348, but further west than the end of the slot it diverged to a slightly more westerly alignment, before petering out on slightly lower ground in a shallow butt-end; this part of the ditch was 24m long with the terminal around 11m to the west of Structure 4. This change in alignment appears to have occurred because of the presence of ditch F379 in this exact position and suggests that the Roman ditch was still evident as a slight depression subsequently utilised by the excavators of F115. At the eastern end the gully turned a sharp right-angle north-eastwards around the postulated corner of Structure 4, extending for a further 5m where it terminated in a definite squared-off end. Its width varied between 0.30 and 0.50m, and the sides sloped steeply onto a curved base, 0.20m deep.

At various points along its length it was cut by field ditches F3 and F302. Its relation to pit F344 was difficult to determine in the field due to the precise similarity of fills and remains ambiguous, but the recorded evidence suggests that

25

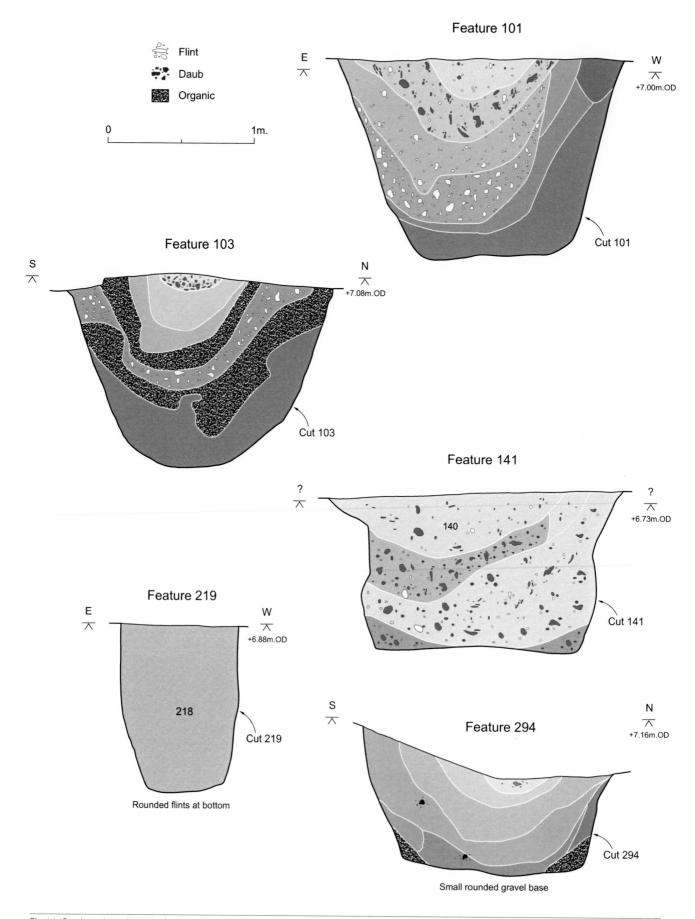

Fig 11. Sections through Anglo-Saxon features F101, F103, F141, F219 and F294.

it was the later feature. The gully also cut a number of Roman features, including the masonry walls of Structure 1.

The fill of the cut (114) varied along its length; it consisted in the main part of dark grey, moderately compacted silty-clay with inclusions of daub, charcoal, tile, animal bone and flint. The abundance of the charcoal and daub inclusions increased (becoming frequent) towards the easterly section of the ditch, nearest to the structure immediately to the north-east, which suggests that the material derived from the occupation of the building. Apart from residual Roman ceramics, one sherd of mid Anglo-Saxon pottery was recovered; a few later sherds (dated to c AD 1050–1175) are now considered to be intrusive, derived from later field ditches and a buried soil which sealed the gully. One other find of probable Anglo-Saxon provenance was a fibre processing spike (*see* p 53).

The arrangement of ditch F115 around Structure 4 and its proximity to the wall line suggest that it was primarily a drain and/or eaves drip gully relating to the building, although it could also have served as an enclosure around the structure. The former interpretation is probably the more likely as it was not found in the trench to the north, and it does not form such an obvious relationship with the pits to the west, as did the ditches of Enclosure 3.

Lying about 6m south-west of Structure 4 was Feature F300, a vertical-sided cut, 2.35m deep and slightly oval in plan in the upper part, the lower section a shaft approximately 0.70m square. The lower part of the cut may have originally been lined with timber planking, long decayed away, and the feature itself probably represents a well. It was filled by a dark brown silty-clay (299), containing rare charcoal, stone and organic inclusions. The date of the feature is problematic. The fill yielded a small quantity of Roman pottery, but also sherds of early thirteenth-century date thought to be intrusive from ditch F99, which truncated its upper fill. From the environmental evidence however, the presence of large quantities of oats and barley would be more consistent with an Anglo-Saxon date (*see* pp 68–69). On balance, it remains possible that the well originated during the Roman phase of occupation, part of the fill at least having been deposited in the Anglo-Saxon phase (Fig 4).

The western pit group

A group of at least thirteen pits and a possible quarry (F413) were located mostly to the west of the Roman Enclosure 2 (although at least two of the features cut the backfilled Roman ditch). Of these, about 60 per cent were half excavated.

The quarry F413 was an irregular but generally oval cut, 7.5m long north to south and about 4m wide. Much of its southern extent had been removed by ditch F99. It appeared to cut the ditches of both Roman enclosures (1 and 2) and was possibly cut by one of the pits (F296 below). A small

section excavated on the western edge revealed a stepped profile, with a flat base cut onto the surface of natural gravels, 0.85m deep. The fill (412) was a very compact, mid orange-yellow-brown silty-clay with very occasional charcoal flecks, but few other inclusions or finds apart from a relatively large amount of mainly Roman pottery.

The exact function or date of this feature remains unclear and it was quite unlike any of the other pits examined; its size suggests that it may have been a quarry or extraction pit but this is by no means certain. Stratigraphy suggests a post-Roman origin, and it has been included in this phase on that basis, although its relation with F296 suggests that it was earlier than that feature and perhaps the remainder of the group.

Pit F274 to the west of the main area of excavation was a near square cut, measuring 1.1 by 1.2m; it was 0.33m deep with a vertical-sided and flat-based profile. The fill (273) was a dark grey-brown silty-clay with inclusions of flints, daub, charcoal and one struck flint flake fragment.

Pit F280, situated a few metres to the east was circular in plan with a diameter of 1.10m and edges that sloped near vertically onto a rounded base, 0.62m deep. The fill (279) was a mid grey-brown silty-clay, with some animal bone, flint and daub inclusions. One organic-tempered Anglo-Saxon sherd was also present as well as loomweight fragments (*see* p 51).

Pit F282, was square cut with rounded corners of side length 1.25m, just to the south-west of F280. It was in excess of 0.90m deep with vertical sides, stained green (it was not fully excavated due to water incursion). The fill (281) was a mid grey-brown silty-clay with patches of yellow clay throughout. The inclusions were charcoal, flint pebble and degraded bone. The staining on the edges suggested that it was a cess-pit.

Pit F286 slightly to the east, was a circular cut of 1.55m diameter. Its western edge cut F288.[9] It was excavated to a depth of 1.10m, though was not bottomed; the sides were near vertical. The fill (285) was a mid greyish-brown, firm, silty-clay, containing inclusions of charcoal, considerable daub, some with wattle impressions and surfaces and rounded pebbles. One Roman tile and a few sherds of Roman pottery were also recovered, but these were probably residual as two Anglo-Saxon sherds were found in association. Its shape and profile were similar to those of the eastern cess-pit group, though there was no evidence of any staining on its sides.

Feature F294 had been completely truncated from above by ditch F99 and only 0.65m of its depth remained (Fig 11). It was circular with a diameter of 1.80m. It cut onto the surface of natural gravels, with a vertical-sided and flat-based profile. The fill (293) represented a number of deposits, consisting in the main of grey silty-clay with charcoal inclusions, layered with yellow-brown redeposited brickearth. At the base of the cut were grey-green cess-type deposits. It was otherwise completely sterile. This, the profile, and staining on the edges of the pit, suggests it was a cess-pit.

---

9.   F288 was an oval pit, cut by feature F286 on its eastern edge. It measured 0.70m in width and would have exceeded 0.87m in length. It was only 0.09m deep with an unremarkable fill and was sufficiently different to the other features here to suggest that it was of a completely different, but earlier, period.

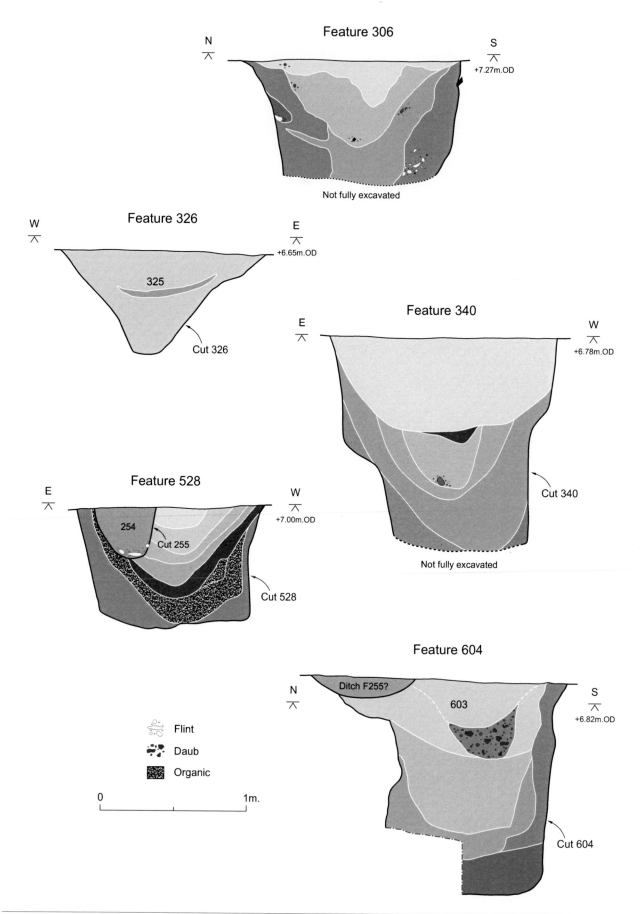

Fig 12. Sections through Anglo-Saxon features F306, F326, F340, F528 and F604.

Further south, Pit F304 was oval, 2m long by 1.7m wide with a very steep-sided profile in excess of 1.20m deep (the feature was not excavated to its full depth). The fill (303) comprised five different deposits, the lowest of which was a mid dark brown silty-clay with charcoal inclusions sealed by a mid light orange-brown silty-clay with stone and charcoal inclusions. Above this was a layer of dark brown silty-clay banded with higher concentrations of charcoal and small flints, underlying an orange silty-clay with pebble and flint. The uppermost fill was a mid dark grey-brown silty-clay with charcoal, daub and stone inclusions. All these deposits exhibited considerable slumping. This and the fact that the sides of the cut were stained green suggest that the feature had also been used as a cess-pit.

The southernmost excavated pit F306 cut the fill of Roman Enclosure 2 ditch F302. It was an approximately circular cut 1.50m in diameter (Fig 12). The sides were vertical, and the base was in excess of 0.85m deep (the feature was not bottomed). The fill (305) consisted of five slumped deposits. These consisted of grey-brown and brown silty-clays containing varying proportions of flints and carbon. The lower deposits appeared to have a high organic or cess content. A layer of redeposited brickearth lined the sides of the pit. Some animal bone, daub, and one sherd of Roman pottery were also recovered. The profile of the feature and the apparent organic content of the fills suggest that it was a cess-pit.

The unexcavated pits (F261, F296, F609, F611 and F613) are almost certainly of the same phase as those described, mainly for topographical reasons.

These features were of varying size and depth, and more varied than the pits within Anglo-Saxon Enclosure 3 to the east. However, the sequence of backfills, virtually sterile artefactually, often demonstrated similarities; there was sometimes heavy greenish staining of the edges of the cut, and a high organic content to some of the deposits. These factors suggested that some of the features at least were used as cess-pits. Others however (such as F274) were of a totally different morphology. If this has not merely been a result of excessive truncation, it may indicate a chronological difference between some of these features, or at least between this group and the compact group to the east. However, a clear north-west/south-easterly alignment of some of the pits (from F609 to the north to F304 or F306 to the south) suggests contemporaneity, or at least a continuous occupational timespan.

Period 4: medieval and post-medieval

There was no artefactual or other evidence for any late Anglo-Saxon occupation of the site and the next phase of activity occurs in the early medieval period, dated by the ceramics to c AD 1050–1150 (Fig 8).

This activity consisted of the three north-east/south-west aligned ditches (F308, F3 and F21) and a short length of (unexcavated) ditch at a near right-angle (F9). These appear to be the latest (apart from modern) features on the site and cut features of most previous phases but were not superseded by any other intrusive feature.

Ditch F308 was the most north-westerly and was traced for a length of over 25m; its maximum width was 0.90m. It extended beyond the site boundary to the north-east, and terminated, with a rounded end to the south-west, but this was considered to be due to later truncation. A 4m long section was excavated, revealing a U-shaped section, with edges sloping onto an uneven base of maximum depth 0.20m. The fill (307/361) was a mixture of yellow-brown redeposited brickearth and grey-brown silty-clay. Inclusions were of daub and charcoal pieces and residual Roman pottery. Also within the fill was part of a circular loomweight (see p 51).

Ditch F3 was located nearly 7m to the south-east on an exactly similar alignment. It extended further south-west than F308 where it terminated similarly; it was traced over a length of over 35m and to the north-east extended out of the site area. The feature was just over 1m wide at maximum but varied considerably in profile and depth, particularly where it cut through Structure 1, where it was much deeper (0.5m) and wider; for some reason much of the masonry of the building had been removed during the cutting of this section of the ditch. This was possibly the result of the necessity of quarrying out parts of the structure to cut the ditch, or perhaps natural curiosity. The fill consisted of a mid grey brown silty-clay (242), which yielded the largest corpus of early medieval pottery from the entire site (see p 44). A similar distance further south-east was another parallel ditch F21, similar to F3 and F308, but only 0.65m wide and 0.35m deep at maximum. Truncation had separated the feature into two lengths.

The ditches were possibly associated with a buried soil (82/268) although the stratigraphic relation between them was impossible to determine. The layer, partially removed by machine, consisted of a spread of what has been interpreted as an old topsoil or agricultural soil that generally survived in the central part of the site, mostly to the north of modern ditch F99. Its north-eastern extent was not determined; its south-western extent was a few metres south-west of Roman enclosure ditch F302, while to the south-east it extended as far as the Anglo-Saxon Enclosure 3. It was c 0.10 to 0.15m thick and consisted of a mid grey brown moderate to very firm silty-clay loam with some Roman tile and charcoal inclusions and a few sherds of pottery of similar date to those from the ditches as well as a considerable amount of residual Roman pottery and a smaller quantity of Anglo-Saxon finds. It sealed all of the previously described Roman and post-Roman deposits in this area.

This layer was in turn sealed by a deposit of reworked brickearth of possibly alluvial origin, or the result of cultivation (1000). Although not systematically excavated, it appeared to be relatively sterile, and may date to fairly recent times. It was cut by the post-medieval or recent ditch F99, which bisected the entire site on a south-east to north-westerly alignment, and which was over 1m deep in places.

3
The Finds

The lithic assemblage

Tania Wilson and John McNabb

Lithic artefacts were recovered during all phases of archaeological fieldwork relating to the construction of the Wainscott by-pass. The total assemblage comprises three main components: unstratified artefacts recovered from various points along the route (including those collected during the gas pipe watching brief); a small assemblage from the Park Pale Farm area; and the assemblage from the Four Elms roundabout excavation and its immediate vicinity.

All of the artefacts have been fully recorded and the catalogue is held with the site archive. The method for recording the dimensions follows Saville's recommendations (Saville 1980, 16) and the cores have been categorised in accordance with Clark's classification (Clark *et al* 1960, 216). In addition to the systematically flaked cores there are also a number of fragmentary cores which are recorded as such, and a quantity of sparsely flaked nodules which are recorded simply as struck nodules or lumps. The dimensions of the cores, as quoted in this text, refer to the maximum dimension in each plane. The term chip is used here to describe complete flakes of 15mm or less in length.

Unstratified artefacts

As can be seen in Table 1, the majority of this group consists of debitage, including two fragmentary blades, two cores and two struck lumps. The retouched pieces include a possible

	Unstratified finds	Park Pale Farm	Four Elms Roundabout
Blades	2	2	22
Irregular knapping debris	1	0	7
Cores and struck lumps	4	1	8
Unimodified flakes and chips	24	9	266
Hammerstones	0	1	0
Biface	1	0	0
Retouched pieces	4	4	33
Total	36	17	336

Table 1. Lithic assemblage: distribution and composition

piercer with minimal retouch, an end retouched scraper and a subtriangular piece (Fig 13, FN 6) with bifacial flaking. The biface described below is of particular significance.

Middle Pleistocene biface
John McNabb

A biface of Middle Pleistocene age was found unstratified as a surface find during fieldwalking (NGR TQ 7043 6983; Tania Wilson, pers comm; Fig 13, FN 8). In form, this kind of biface was not produced during the Holocene. While it may date to the Late Pleistocene, it is probably best located in the Middle Pleistocene. Archaeologically this would be the equivalent of the Lower Palaeolithic or early Middle Palaeolithic (*sensu* post-Levallois first appearance datum in Oxygen/Isotope stage 8; Bridgland 1998).

Typology

Since the tip of the artefact has broken off it is difficult to be certain as to what category within current classifications of biface shape it should be placed in. In the Roe (1968) system the biface would likely be a pointed one, occupying the right hand section of his tripartite diagrams.

On the Bordes system (1961) the piece would be classed as a thick biface (m/e <2.35, value = 1.854), either a lanceolate or a ficron (*sensu* Bordes with sinuous edges and *contra* British usage which is with concave edges). I am inclined to assign it to the ficron class since, although broken, the tip appears to lack the more careful thinning and shaping usually associated with the lanceolate in this classification. The edges are markedly sinuous in profile.

On the Wymer (1985) system the biface, reconstructed, would be a pointed one (F) with a part cortical butt (a), a pointed tip (ii or iii), and straight/sinuous edges (e).

Condition

The biface is rolled and shows innumerable small damage scars along its edges, and characteristically on thick obtuse angles. Whether or not the rolling damage is actually a result of immersion and transport in a fluvial environment, or is a result of damage incurred as a surface/buried artefact is

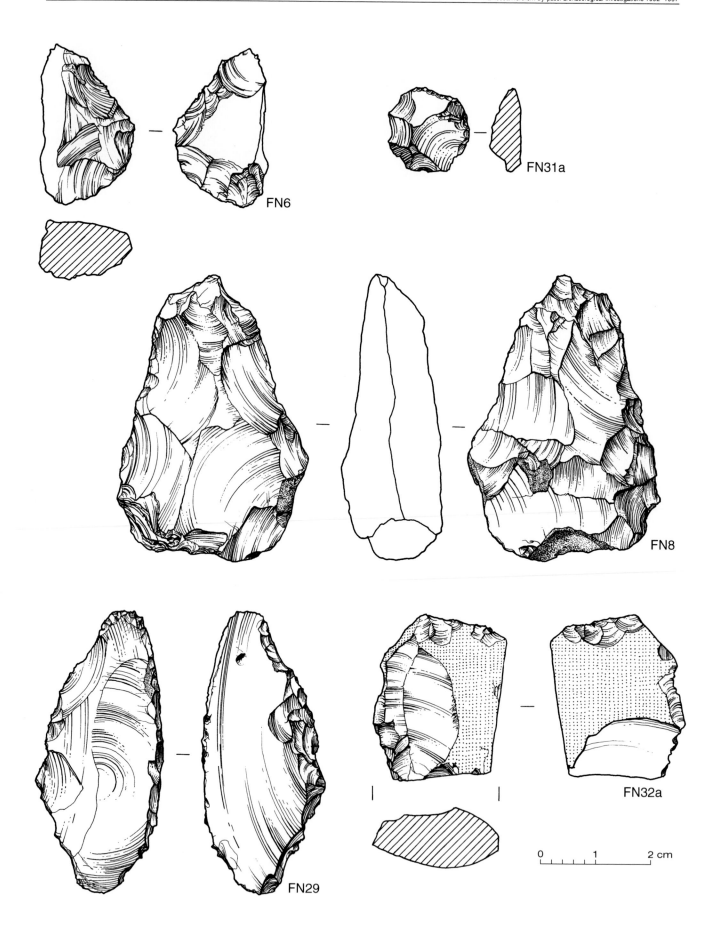

Fig 13. Lithics. Scale 1:2.

impossible to ascertain. More recent damage scars have been picked out by differential patination and appear grey in colour.

The piece is also patinated and stained. The patination takes the form of the common blue background with white basket work linear patterning. Also a common feature is the fact that one face is darker blue than the other which is a white/grey/light blue colour. This may indicate that this face is in a more advanced state of patination reflecting the circumstances of which face was in contact with groundwater or the air. A thin wash of brown staining has covered the majority of both faces, and is as usual more developed away from the cortex. The combination of brown thin staining and patination underneath gives the biface the characteristic green tinge of flints that are associated with chalklands.

Technology

The presence of cortex on both faces indicates that the biface was made of a nodule of flint. Only a minimal amount of working is present on the still cortical butt. Although the piece has the appearance of being made with a hard hammer (and probably was) this cannot be asserted with total confidence. There are thick areas on the lateral edges, one very near the broken tip region. Adjacent to this and cutting into it slightly are a series of piled up step fractures, whose patination and staining suggest they are ancient in character. Despite being reconstructed as a long pointed biface these step fractures may indicate that the piece broke during manufacture and these represent an attempt by the knapper to salvage the biface and produce a serviceable tip.

Park Pale Farm

This assemblage although quite small includes, alongside the waste material, one incomplete core and a core rejuvenation flake. This flake has an area of crushing on the dorsal surface which suggests that the core may also have been used as a hammerstone. Four retouched pieces were also collected from this area. One piece (Fig 14, FN 36) possibly best

described as a knife, has been made on a blade-like flake with abrupt retouch along the left-hand side and, abundant chipping along the right-hand side may be consistent with utilisation damage. One large flake (Fig 13, FN 29) with some bifacial flaking was recovered, and a fine end scraper (Fig 14, FN 32b) with semi-abrupt retouch was also collected. Of particular note is a possible fabricator (Fig 14, FN 33), which is unfortunately incomplete.

Four Elms Roundabout

Waste material

A total of 265 waste flakes were collected from this site, weighing just over 2.5kg; 61.5 per cent of the flakes are complete. Small quantities of other knapping debris were also recovered. The dimensions of the complete flakes and chips from this area are summarised in Table 2. Twenty-two blades were collected, of which half are complete. Only 2 per cent of the flakes are primary or preparation flakes, the remainder almost equally split between secondary and tertiary flakes.

A total of eight cores and struck nodules were collected during this excavation. The quantities of the different core types and their weights are shown in Table 3. The maximum measurements range from 32mm to 112mm, with an average of 54mm. The majority of the cores have three or more platforms (eg FN 632a and FN 645a, Fig 14). One exception is a blade core (Fig 14, FN 677) which, whilst having two platforms, still however retains a vague pyramidal form. In addition, this core has a crushed area where a number of flakes terminate, which may be an indication that it was struck on an anvil. Many of the cores are struck on flawed material; some examples show that previously shattered flint was selected for use whilst other pieces suggest that the core may have shattered during flaking.

Evidence of core preparation is sparse throughout this assemblage. Where it could be determined only 6 per cent of the flakes and 6 per cent of the blades have faceted or dihedral striking platforms. Slightly more preparation appears to have gone into blade production as 23 per cent

	0–9mm	10–19mm	20–29mm	30–39mm	40–49mm	50–59mm	60–69mm	>70mm
Length	0	10	31	26	23	6	3	1
Breadth	1	13	37	28	16	3	1	1
Thickness	59	40	1	0	0	0	0	0

Table 2. Dimensions of complete flakes and chips from the Four Elms site (figures in per cent).

	Class of core									
	A1	A2	B1	B2	B3	C	D	E	Fragment	Struck lump/ nodule
Quantity	*	*	1	1	*	4	*	*	1	1
Total weight	*	*	117	27	*	152	*	*	19	363
Average weight	*	*	117	27	*	38	*	*	19	363

Table 3. Cores from the Four Elms site (weight in grams).

show evidence of platform abrasion, as opposed to only 5 per cent of the flakes.

Retouched pieces

Thirty-three retouched pieces were retrieved from this site, and these are summarised in Table 4. As the table shows, most of the retouched pieces are either scrapers (eg Fig 13, FN 31a, Fig 14, FN 622, FN 631c and FN 668) or retouched flakes which have fairly limited retouch usually located towards the distal end. In total, the retouched pieces form 10 per cent of the assemblage.

Type	Quantity
Axe (ground and polished)	1
Gun flint	1
Retouched flakes	16
Notch	1
Piercers	3
Scrapers	11

Table 4. Retouched pieces from the Four Elms site.

The majority (seven) of the scrapers are of the end-and-side retouched form, whilst the remainder are retouched at the distal end only. Of the end-and-side retouched pieces, most are retouched along one side only. The dimensions of the complete scrapers are shown in Table 5. The average length is 45mm, the average breadth is 41mm and the thickness is 14mm; in general, therefore, they tend to be almost as wide as they are long and are made on fairly slender flakes.

Three pieces which have been broadly classified as piercers were collected. One has abrupt retouch on both sides forming a point at the distal end and one example (Fig 14, FN 743) has fairly limited semi-abrupt retouch at the distal end of a blade-like flake. The third is unusual in the fact that it has been retouched to form a point at the bulbar end, this retouch having completely removed the striking platform.

Only one possibly notched piece (Fig 14, FN 673) was recovered. This piece is formed on a now incomplete blade and has two concave areas of retouch located towards the bulbar end on opposing sides.

The most significant artefact is a fragment of a ground and polished axe (Fig 13, FN 32a), which has been broken and flaked in antiquity. Only the cutting end of the axe survives, but it can be seen that the axe had an oval section with flattened sides. A grey flint with opaque inclusions was selected for the production of this piece.

Raw material and condition

The majority of the lithics, regardless of provenance or stratification, are in a fresh, unpatinated condition. There are a few examples with some patination and a small amount is burnt. Several pieces, including those recovered from features, have evidence of post-depositional damage, possibly caused by later activities and/or farming practices.

The raw material selected for use consists of a wide range of flint types including black, grey, orange/brown and glauconitic (Bullhead) flint; all types often contain opaque, almost cherty inclusions. Most of these types are represented in relatively small quantities but a grey/brown semi-translucent flint dominates in both the assemblage from the excavation and the artefacts from elsewhere. The cortex, where present, is generally buff coloured, hard and weathered.

Raw material for flintworking appears to have been selected from surface nodules. The condition of the cortex suggests that whilst the flint was originally derived from the chalk, the nodules had probably become eroded out of the chalk prior to selection. Furthermore, there appears to be some evidence for the selection of frost-shattered material, which may also indicate surface collection.

Technology

Consideration of the Wainscott assemblage as a whole shows that, with the exception of the biface, the technological attributes of the material from each component discussed above are quite similar. In general, flake production appears to be preferred and hard hammer percussion dominates throughout. Cores with several striking platforms are the most common and, whilst there is some evidence for core preparation and rejuvenation, this is in the minority. There appears to be no preference in the type of blank selected for the production of retouched pieces, or indeed the type of raw material.

Overall there appears to be little care for an economical approach to flintworking, which probably reflects the good availability of raw material. In addition the evidence for the use of flawed raw material demonstrates little desire for the sole use of good quality flint.

Conclusions

The lithic artefacts recovered during all phases of this project clearly demonstrate activity across this area prior to the Roman activity shown at the Four Elms site. Whilst it is clear that the artefacts collected along the route are residual, their

	0–9mm	10–19mm	20–29mm	30–39mm	40–49mm	50–59mm	60–69mm
Length	0	0	0	25	62.5	0	12.5
Breadth	0	0	0	50	37.5	0	12.5
Thickness	25	62.5	12.5	0	0	0	0

Table 5. Dimensions of complete scrapers from the Four Elms site (figures in per cent).

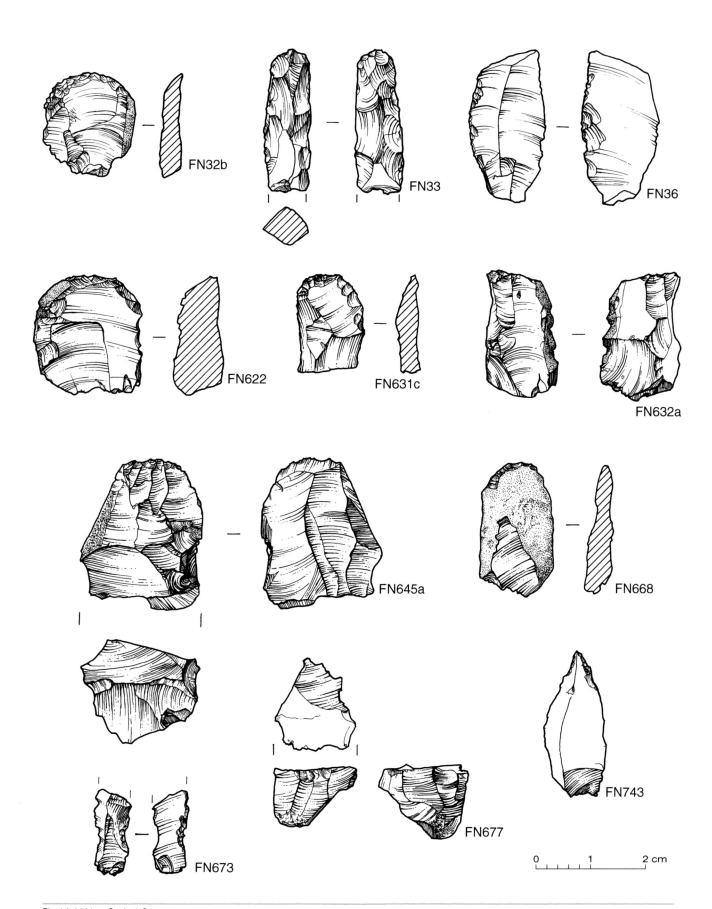

Fig 14. Lithics. Scale 1:2.

general condition implies that they have not moved very far from their original place of deposition.

Consideration of both the typological pieces and some of the technological attributes suggests that two distinct phases of activity may be represented within the study area. The earliest phase of activity is represented by the biface, dating to the Lower or Middle Palaeolithic. This artefact appears to be a solitary find.

The composition and condition of the bulk of the assemblage suggests that the remaining artefacts are broadly contemporary and, based upon pieces such as the fabricator and the ground and polished axe fragment, it is likely that a late Neolithic to early Bronze Age date is represented. The quantity and concentration of this group at the Four Elms site may suggest a focus of activity dating to this period and, given the relatively high proportion of retouched pieces, it is possible that this assemblage represents domestic activities taking place within the immediate vicinity. Equally the small yet significant assemblage from the Park Pale Farm area may also indicate similar activities.

Previous discoveries within the area of the by-pass are relatively scarce. The nearest material contemporary with the biface are the assemblages discovered at Frindsbury and at Cuxton, both situated to the south of the study area and close to the River Medway. These assemblages consist of substantial quantities of debitage and bifaces (Cruse 1987, 43; Tester 1965, 30; Wheatley 1926, 183). Neolithic and Bronze Age evidence is equally scarce, with one published note relating to a polished flint axe and an edge-ground knife from Higham (Cook 1936, 234) and, a bronze dagger found in the River Medway at Chatham Reach, Frindsbury (Kelly 1987).

Evidence for prehistoric activity within the area of the Wainscott by-pass has hitherto been relatively sparse. However, the flint assemblage recovered during these excavations has provided evidence of Lower to Middle Palaeolithic activity some distance from the River Medway and for possible settlements of Neolithic to Bronze Age date.

Later prehistoric pottery

Nigel Macpherson-Grant

Thirty-one prehistoric sherds (weighing 112g) were recovered. With the exception of one undiagnostic sherd from F340 (a pit to the south of Structure 3, Period 3; not discussed here), all the material recovered is Middle Bronze Age pottery in the Deverel-Rimbury tradition. Most of this comes from residual contexts except for a single pit F270 (Period 1).

The assemblage is small and consists mainly of small sherds, with the exception of that from F270, which contains medium-sized sherds and fragmentary scraps from F278 (a later Roman pit, Period 2). Overall, the sherds exhibit a mixed wear pattern, ranging from heavily worn to fresh, the majority being moderately worn.

The assemblage

Fabrics

Fabric types were identified using a x10 hands lens and broadly equated with regional fabric types on the basis of the main deliberate and/or naturally occurring elements (eg fabrics 4 and 14). Most fabrics have silt-grade matrices or contain sparse-moderate quantities of natural organic and ferrous-oxide inclusions; these are not normally indicated unless they are the visually dominant ingredient (eg Fabric 15) or considered to indicate a potentially significant different source than the normal site range (eg fabrics containing profuse inclusions of iron-oxide). Obviously intentional filler types are italicised. The fabrics recorded are summarised on a period basis in Table 6.

Fabric	Quantity
LBA 4: *flint-tempered*	25
LBA 11: *flint-tempered*, moderate–profuse quartz	1
LBA 14: *flint-tempered and moderate–profuse organic inclusions*	1
LBA 15: *flint-tempered*, moderate–profuse iron oxides	1
LBA 16: *flint-tempered and sparse–moderate grog inclusions*	2

Table 6. Prehistoric pottery fabric types and sherd frequencies.

In terms of fabric types, Table 6 is self-evident: all fabrics contain flint-temper, and the only noteworthy aspect is the mixed-temper fabrics LBA 14 and LBA 16. Throughout, filler quantities are moderate to profuse, with a consistent size range of <1mm for finewares: coarsewares have larger filler grades between 1–2mm with the exception of a storage jar body sherd which has grits up to 10mm. The organic component of LBA 14 appears visually profuse as fine black streaks averaging 2–3mm in length; the crushed grog inclusions in fabric LBA 16 average between 1–2mm. Most fabrics have fine silty matrices with few other naturally occurring inclusions. Exceptions to these are the notably different natural content of Fabrics 14 and 16; overall this suggests the likelihood that three different clay sources were used.

Wall thickness, surface finishes and firing trends

These manufacturing aspects are difficult to assess due to the size and condition of the assemblage. However, it is worth noting that wall thickness sizes range from 10–12mm for coarsewares while finewares average 5mm. Finewares mostly exhibit even surfaces and the overall impression is of an assemblage dominated by reduced firing trends, with only one or two partially oxidised vessels.

Vessel and decoration types

Fineware vessel types are represented mostly by body sherds from globular jars or bowls, with the exception of

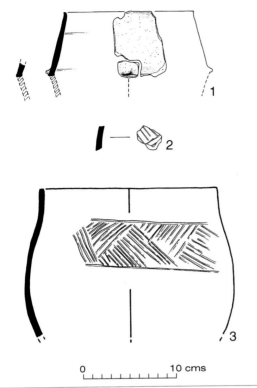

Fig 15. Middle Bronze Age pottery. No 1, Period 1, F270; No 2, Period 2, F302. No 3, suggested reconstruction, No 2. Scale 1:4.

the more complete example from F270 (Fig 15.1). This is a globular jar, which has between two to four simple applied small, unperforated lugs, placed horizontally around the body. For coarsewares, a bucket or barrel-type storage jar is represented by a single sherd from F270; all other body sherds are probably from smaller jars or tubs.

Other than the vestigial lugs on No 1, the only other decorative element is a sherd (Fig 15.2) from (424), the fill of F302 (Enclosure 2, Period 2). This was in Fabric LBA 16 with decoration consisting of shallow-tooled opposed filled triangles, similar to material from Kimpton, Hampshire (Dacre and Ellison 1981, fig 15, D/E6; a reconstruction of the Wainscott vessel based on the Kimpton find is presented as Fig 15.3).

Production quality

This analytical aspect is difficult to assess because the overall condition of the assemblage is generally poor. However, fineware flint fillers are consistently fine and well-sorted and the sherds are frequently thin-walled, suggesting potting clays and vessel production, for finewares at least, were imbued with a sense of quality. In contrast to this is No 2 in Fabric LBA 16, with lightly tooled, but rather haphazard decoration which is interestingly mirrored in examples from Kimpton.

Dating

Though this is a small assemblage, both Nos 1 and 2 are from vessel types that are typical of the middle Bronze Age

Deverel-Rimbury tradition, particularly from the south and south-east of England, the dating of which has recently been re-assessed (on the basis of metalwork associated radiocarbon dates), with the main *floruit* between 1500–1150 cal BC (Needham 1996, figs 2–3, Period 5). Within this span, the decorated sherd No 2 can be usefully linked to the radiocarbon date applied to globular jars from Kimpton phases D and D/E (1590–1290 cal BC). Phase D of the same site has a lugged jar (similar to No 1) which can be further linked to the two radiocarbon dates for the recent small assemblage from Dartford (Couldrey 2003, 55–9). With these in mind, the slim set of parallels for Wainscott suggest that the latter can also be placed fairly early within the tradition, ie between *c* 1500–1200 BC.

Roman pottery

Malcolm Lyne

The site yielded a total of 2,951 sherds of third-century pottery (weighing 30,177g) with most of it coming from Structure 1 and Enclosure 2 Ditch F41 (Period 2). Some of the pottery was residual in later features.

All of the eighty-nine pottery assemblages were quantified by numbers of sherds and their weights per fabric. These fabrics were identified using a x8 magnification lens with built-in metric scale in order to determine the nature, size, frequency and form of added inclusions. Only one assemblage, from Context 40 (a fill of Enclosure 2 ditch F11/41/302), was large enough for more accurate quantification by Estimated Vessel Equivalents (EVEs) based on rim sherds (Orton 1975).

The fabrics

Fabrics were classified using the codes formulated by CAT (Macpherson-Grant *et al* 1995). The following codes are used in Table 7.

B2.2. Local hand-made coarse grog-tempered ware of probable late Roman date.

R13 IMIT. Hand-made coarse-sanded grey fabric with profuse sub-angular multi-coloured quartz filler and occasional larger ironstone inclusions, fired pimply black externally and polished black internally. Imitation Dorset Black-Burnished 1 ware.

R14. Black-Burnished 2 ware from Cliffe and other sources in north Kent.

R16. Wheel-turned Upchurch reduced fineware. Sand-free with soft brown to black argillaceous inclusions.

R17.1. Cream-slipped oxidised Hoo fineware from the Medway estuary. An oxidised version of R16.

R62. Kent Fabric 2 mortaria in very fine-textured orange-brown fabric with cream slip. Probably a Hoo product.

R68. Patchgrove ware.

R73. Very fine-sanded rough grey Thameside grey ware.

R73.1. Similar but with blackened surfaces.

Fabric	Jar	Bowl	Dish	Beaker	Storage jar	Others	Total	%
B2.2	P						P	
R13 IMIT			0.38				0.38	3.30
R14		0.54	0.78				1.32	11.60
R16		0.05					0.05	0.40
R17.1						Flagon 0.46	0.46	4.00
R62						Mortarium P	P	
R68				P			P	
R73	0.93	0.01		0.30			1.24	10.90
R73.1	4.95	0.59	0.29		0.08		5.91	51.90
R74.1	0.33	0.13	0.17				0.63	5.50
R99						Mortarium 0.10	0.10	0.90
LR1.1	P						P	
LR2.2	0.21	0.10					0.31	2.70
LR5.1	0.35						0.35	3.10
LR7						Mortarium 0.10	0.10	0.90
LR10			0.28	0.15			0.43	3.80
LR11				0.10			0.10	0.90
Total	6.77	1.42	1.90	0.55	0.08	0.66	11.38	
Percentage	59.50	12.50	16.70	4.80	0.70	5.80		

Table 7. Frequency of Roman pottery fabrics and vessel forms by EVEs. P: present.

R74.1. An oxidised version of Fabric R73.

R99. Miscellaneous mortarium fabric fired reddish-brown with silt-sized to 0.10mm quartz filler and crushed flint trituration grits.

LR1.1. Late Roman hand-made grog-tempered ware with pale siltstone grog.

LR2.2. Pale grey gritty fabric with up to 0.50mm multi-coloured quartz filler, fired rough darker grey with superficial surface reddening. A late Thameside fabric.

LR5.1. Alice Holt/Farnham type grey ware but rather hard and coarse. Probably from a more local source such as the Preston kiln(s) in east Kent.

LR7. Oxfordshire Whiteware.

LR10. Oxfordshire red/brown colour-coat wares.

LR11. Lower Nene Valley colour-coat wares.

The assemblages

Assemblage 1

From constructional contexts relating to Structure 1.

Almost all constructional contexts relating to Structure 1 were totally lacking in pottery. The eastern wall of the later flue inserted in the north-west corner of the structure (F85) did, however, have four sherds of pottery incorporated in it, including the following piece:

A small rim fragment from a dish of Monaghan Type 5F3.9 (1987), c AD 170–230. This sherd dates the construction of the flue to after c AD 170 and probably to the early third century. Two of the other sherds are in Thameside grey ware of late second- to third-century character and the fourth is a somewhat abraded chip from a North Kent Shell-tempered storage jar (c AD 50–170; not illustrated).

Assemblage 2

From the lower fills within Structure 1: (399 and 500, primary use; 388 and 393, flue collapse; 93, 94, 96, 370, 428, 438, 440, 441, 442, 459 and 470, collapse of Structure 1 and dumping).

These lower fills were for the most part lacking in pottery. A single flagon fragment from the primary ash deposit in the north-western flue (500) can only be dated generally to the period c AD 50–250. An overlying silty ash (399) and a later infill layer (442) contained only four very broken up sherds of third- to early fourth-century date. Three more substantial fills above these in Structure 1 (428, 438 and 439) produced only three further sherds, of probable third- to early fourth-century date. The later fills of the flue (388 and 393) and (93, 94, 96 and 370) were not much more productive: the five sherds recovered do, however, include three large, fresh jar sherds from context 393 in Thameside grey ware with a watery external white slip; suggestive of a post AD 270 date.

Assemblage 3

From an upper fill of the Structure 1 stoke-hole (345) and associated drainage system, overlying the deposits containing Assemblage 4.

The stoke-hole produced eighty-four sherds (weighing 1,660g) including one tiny fragment each of ?South Gaulish samian and a Lower Nene Valley colour-coat beaker (c AD 180–300), as well as the following pieces:

Fig 16.1. Much of jar with rolled over rim, in grey Thameside fabric R73. Similar to Oakleigh Farm kilns type GFXVI.VTi (Catherall 1983), c AD 250–300+.

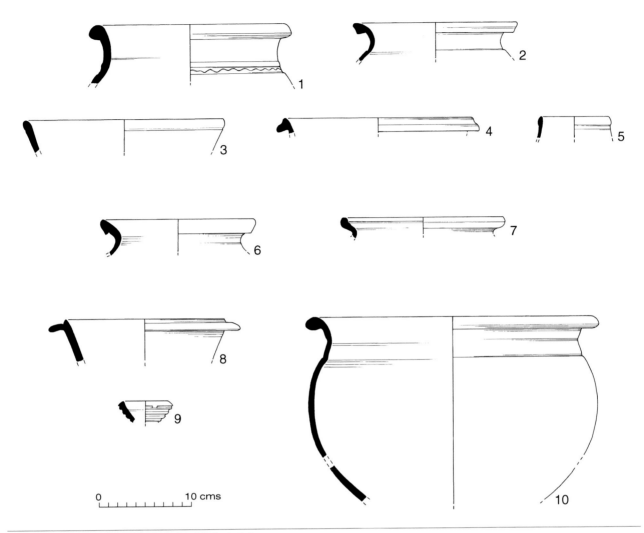

Fig 16. Roman pottery. Assemblages 3, 4 and 5. Scale 1:4.

Fig 16.2. Everted-rim jar with moulded rim, in similar fabric with superficial surface reddening.

Fig 16.3. Bead-rim dish in dark-grey rough Thameside fabric R73.1 with localised reddened patches. Monaghan (1989) dates the type to *c* AD 130–230, but the form was present in Kiln A at Oakleigh Farm, which is manifestly later than AD 250 in date (Catherall 1983, 12-8). A latest date of *c* AD 250–70 seems more likely for the type.

Fig 16.4. Developed beaded-and-flanged bowl in similar fabric. Similar to Pollard's type 190 (1988, fig 49), *c* AD 250–350.

Fig 16.5. Bead-rim beaker in similar fabric. *c* AD 250–350.

The presence of a small 'pie dish' fragment (*c* AD 170–270) alongside these types suggests a date of *c* AD 270 for this assemblage and thus for the abandonment of the drier.

Assemblage 4

From the upper fills (444/448) of drain F430/445 on the southern and western sides of Structure 1.

These fills produced twenty-five sherds (254g) of pottery, much of which is freshly broken and includes:

Fig 16.6. Jar of Monaghan type 3H5-2 (1987) in reddish-brown Thameside fabric R73 fired rough medium grey. *c* AD 250–300. (444).

Fig 16.7. Lid-seated jar in similar fabric and similar to Oakleigh Farm kilns type GFXI VTi associated with Kiln A (Catherall 1983, figs 13–39). One of two. Monaghan dates the type *c* AD 170–230 (1987, Type 2LO-1) and Pollard is in general agreement (1988, Type 201, late second to mid third century).

Assemblage 5

From the upper fills (429, 443 and 89) of drain cuts F90 and F430/F445 on the southern and western sides of Structure 1, overlying the deposits containing Assemblage 4.

The eighty-one sherds (1,108g) of pottery from these three contexts consist overwhelmingly of Thameside grey wares of broadly third- to early fourth-century date and include further fragments from the same beaker as was present in the fills of the drier stoke-hole (Fig 16.5), a

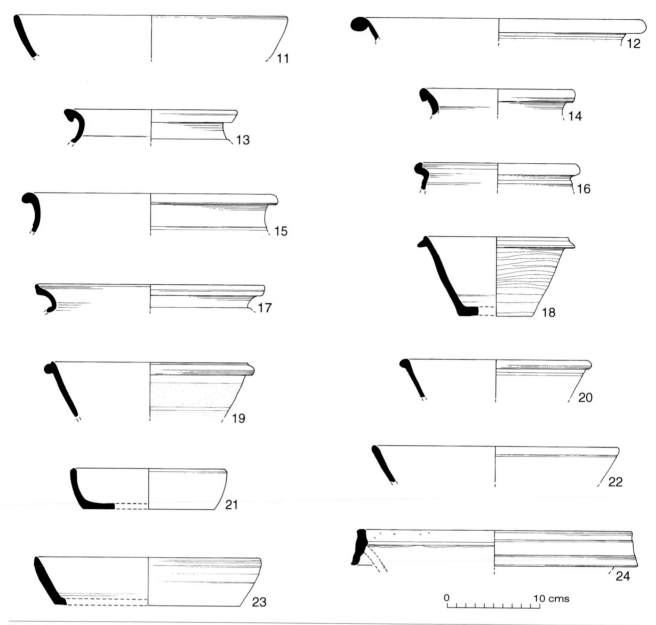

Fig 17. Roman pottery. Assemblage 6. Scale 1:4.

straight-sided dish of third-century type in BB2 fabric, two body sherds from a Patchgrove storage jar (*c* AD 50–270) and the following fragments:

Fig 16.8. Developed beaded-and-flanged bowl in coarse Thameside grey ware with external reddening, copying BB1 prototypes. *c* AD 270–300+. (443).

Fig 16.9. Flagon rim sherd in orange Hoo fabric, of Pollard type 158 (1988), *c* AD 150–250. (89).

Fig 16.10. Necked bowl with rolled over rim, of Monaghan class 4A2 (1987), dated by him to *c* AD 120/170–250. (89).

Assemblage 6

From the fills of Enclosure 2 ditches F11, F41 and F302: (10, 40, 301 and 369).

The fills of Ditches F11 and F302 produced a total of seventy-three sherds (515g) including an Oxfordshire red colour-coat beaker base (*c* AD 240–400), Patchgrove storage jar fragments (*c* AD 50–270) and a few post AD 270 Alice Holt/Farnham grey ware sherds. The rest of the sherds are in a variety of local Thameside grey wares but include only two nondescript jar rim chips. Ditch section F41 was far more productive of pottery: the lower fill (369) produced thirty-six sherds (551g) of pottery, including the following:

Fig 17.11. Convex-sided dish of Monaghan type 5E2-3 in re-fired brown-grey Thameside fabric with patchy internal cream slip. *c* AD 270–350.

The upper fill of the ditch produced the largest pottery assemblage from the site (989 sherds, 11,324g), which is large enough for quantification by Estimated Vessel Equivalents (EVEs) based on rim sherds (Table 7).

The assemblage is entirely dominated by Thameside industry products (75 per cent); not surprising in view of the close proximity of the site to the kilns of that industry. The Oakleigh Farm kilns are situated just over 10 kilometres to the west and the nearest Medway estuary ones only 5 kilometres to the east. The form breakdown of the assemblage is typical of a low status rural site of the period, in being dominated by cooking pots and having very small quantities of fine and specialised wares.

The local Thameside industry wares include the following pieces:

Fig 17.12. Necked bowl with rolled over rim of Monaghan class 4A2 in rough grey Thameside fabric R73.1. One of at least nine examples. Monaghan dates the type to *c* AD 120/170–250 but similar vessels were associated with the mid to late third-century Kiln A at Oakleigh Farm and were present in the *c* AD 270–300 dated pottery group B at Chalk (Johnston 1972, figs 8–12).

Fig 17.13. Hook-rimmed jar of Monaghan type 3H8.1 in similar fabric.. One of six examples, *c* AD 190–300+.

Fig 17.14. Hook-rimmed jar of Monaghan type 3H5.1 in sandy late Thameside fabric LR2.1. *c* AD 270–300+.

Fig 17.15. Jar with rolled over rim of Monaghan type 3H2.7 in grey fabric LR5.1. *c* AD 190–300.

Fig 17.16. Lid-seated jar of Monaghan type 3L4.1 in similar fabric. Dated by Monaghan to *c* AD 190–240 but paralleled in the *c* AD 270–300 dated pottery group B at Chalk (Johnston 1972, figs 8–22).

Fig 17.17. Everted-rim jar in oxidised Thameside fabric R74.1. *c* AD 190–230.

Fig 17.18. Developed beaded-and-flanged bowl in rough grey Thameside fabric R73.1. *c* AD 250–350. One of three.

Fig 17.19. Similar vessel, but with stubby flange, in similar fabric. *c* AD 240–300.

Fig 17.20. 'Pie-dish' of Monaghan type 5C1.5 in similar fabric. *c* AD 170–270.

Fig 17.21. Convex-sided dish of type 5E2.5 in polished black BB2 fabric. Dated to *c* AD 170–230 by Monaghan (1987) but continuing in use until at least AD 300.

Fig 17.22. A straight-sided dish of Monaghan type 5F3.10 in grey fabric LR5.1. *c* AD 130–270.

Most of this assemblage probably accumulated after the end of fine pottery production in Upchurch grey and Hoo white-slipped oxidised orange wares. The few pieces in those fabrics do, however, include the following:

Flagon with flanged rim of Monaghan type 1A5 in orange Hoo fabric R17.1 (not illustrated). *c* AD 190–260. Paralleled at Chalk in the *c* AD 270–300 dated pottery group B (Johnston 1972, figs 10–48).

The non-local sherds include fragments from an Oxfordshire red colour-coat dish of Young type C44 (1977, *c* AD 270–350) and beakers of type C22 and uncertain form (*c* AD 240–400), as well as a mortarium of Young's type M17 (*c* AD 240–300) in Oxfordshire Whiteware. A rim sherd from a Nene Valley colour-coat beaker with beaded rim (*c* AD 250–300) and the following pieces are also present:

Fig 17.23. Straight-sided dish in hand-made coarse grey fabric with profuse sub-angular multi-coloured quartz and occasional larger ironstone filler fired pimply black externally and polished black internally. Sixteen fresh sherds from this dish and another smaller one in the same imitation BB1 fabric are present, *c* AD 270–300.

Fig 17.24. Wall-sided mortarium in bricky reddish-brown fabric with crushed flint and ironstone trituration grits, *c* AD 150–250.

The dating of this pottery is broadly in keeping with that of the associated coinage in suggesting a date of *c* AD 270–300 for the deposition of the assemblage.

Conclusions

The ceramic evidence for the commencement of Roman occupation on the site is somewhat ambiguous. The presence of a truncated North Kent Shell-tempered ware storage jar in pit F278 suggests a date earlier than AD 150/170 but an absence of other exclusively second-century forms from the site may mean that the storage jar was already old when placed in the pit: vessels of that type tend to have a long life in use. The total absence of BB2 'pie-dishes' with latticed decoration and similarly decorated cooking pots so typical of *c* AD 130–200 dated assemblages in west Kent and so close to their source suggests that occupation may have commenced as late as the early years of the third century. An absence of exclusively fourth-century material further suggests that occupation ceased around AD 300 or shortly afterwards.

The residual Roman sherds associated with the Anglo-Saxon and later features form a significant portion of the total site assemblage and have a similar date range to the material stratified in Roman features.

Post-Roman pottery

John Cotter

The post-Roman pottery assemblage is summarised in Table 8. For both the EMS and MLS fabrics the CAT fabric codes used are the same as (or derived from) those first devised for Canterbury (Macpherson-Grant *et al* 1995). However, their use here refers to a tradition of pottery manufacture which, in some cases, was widespread throughout Kent and other areas of Anglo-Saxon England. Most of the pottery described below, unless stated otherwise, is most probably of local manufacture, hand-made and fired in bonfire kilns. Dates given below for the Anglo-Saxon fabrics likewise reflect their known or estimated currency at Canterbury – the nearest settlement where pottery of this period has been studied in depth. The Canterbury dates are at least a useful indicator of the likely currency of similar wares in the Wainscott area. Good typological parallels, particularly for the shelly wares, are also published from the Middle Saxon port of Sandtun, West Hythe, on the south-east coast of Kent (Blackmore 2001; Macpherson-Grant 2001).

Fabric	Period	Quantity	Weight (g)
EMS 4: organic-tempered ware	Early–Mid Saxon	7	42
MLS 4: sparse shell-tempered ware	Mid–Late Saxon	5	47
MLS 4C: fine sandy ware with shell	Mid–Late Saxon	2	32
MLS 5: sandy ware with sparse–moderate shell	Mid–Late Saxon	3	70
MLS 5A: coarse sandy ware with sparse–moderate shell	Mid–Late Saxon	3	81
MLS 7A: Ipswich ware, sandy	Mid–Late Saxon	3	51
EM 1: Canterbury sandy ware	Early Medieval	1	2
EM 2: shelly ware	Early Medieval	24	128
EM 3: shelly-sandy ware	Early Medieval	5	36
Total		53	489

Table 8. Early to Mid Saxon wares (EMS) *c* AD 400–650, Mid to Late Saxon wares (MLS) *c* AD 650–850 and Early Medieval wares (EM) *c* 1050–1225.

Early to Mid Saxon wares (EMS) *c* AD 400–650 and Mid to Late Saxon wares (MLS) *c* AD 650–850

EMS4 Organic-tempered ware *c* AD 575–800. Almost purely organic-tempered (coarse chopped grass or chaff) with a soft, fairly pure or finely sandy 'brickearth' matrix. The organic material is usually burnt-out leaving a corky texture with a laminated fracture. Surfaces have a characteristic smooth soapy feel. Firing colour is generally reduced dark grey or brownish-grey. Light overall internal/external burnishing is common. In other parts of south-east England small quantities of organic-tempered ware are present from the fifth century onwards, becoming the dominant fabric of the sixth–seventh centuries, eg Mucking, Essex (Hamerow 1993, fig 17). At Canterbury and other east Kent sites, eg Minster, Sheppey, the demise of organic-tempered wares seems to coincide or overlap with the introduction of Ipswich ware (currently *c* AD 720–850). In one context at Wainscott (context 343, the fill of pit F351 in the central pit group, Period 3), two joining sherds of organic-tempered ware are associated with a fresh sherd of Ipswich ware. The organic-tempered sherds are lacking their internal surfaces, but are otherwise fresh. This, and the looser association here with Mid-Saxon shell-tempered wares (*c* AD 750–875), could suggest local continuation of the organic-tempered tradition perhaps as late as *c* AD 800. Rims from at least two separate smallish jars were recovered including Fig 18.1.

MLS4 Sparsely shell-tempered ware *c* AD 750–875. Soft, virtually sand-free or silty 'brickearth' matrix (very similar to organic-tempered EMS4), generally reduced dark grey. Sparse fine to coarse shell platelets. Can be partially burnished externally. At Canterbury samples have thin platy shell, possibly oyster, and sparse cockle or scallop. The five sherds from Wainscott are all body sherds from a single jar in a variant fabric. This is reduced with coarse platy shell voids up to 6mm and distinctive sparse, coarse, orange-red iron-stained and iron-coated quartz grains (also noted in some early medieval fabrics in the Medway area). Also abundant fine mica, sparse medium-coarse hard brownish haematite, rare flint, sandstone or ironstone and rare coarse organic inclusions.

MLS4C Fine sandy ware with shell *c* AD 750–875. Similar in appearance/technology to organic-tempered ware (EMS4) but with shell rather than organic temper. Basic, reduced grey, soft, brickearth fabric. Mostly finely sandy, but occasionally with fine–medium quartz and sparse–moderate inclusions of flint, iron oxide, clay pellets and fine mica (abundant here). Moderate to abundant shell voids to 4mm, species unrecognisable in this case. The only identifiable form here is a jar (Fig 18.2) with faint diagonal faceting/construction marks externally. The interior has patches of thick sooting.

MLS5 Sandy ware with sparse-moderate shell *c* AD 700–800. Represented by a jar rim (Fig 18.3) in a dark brownish-grey fabric. Moderate medium–coarse quartz, clear, milky and brown-tinted. Moderate coarse to very coarse shell inclusions, mostly voided or calcined but includes bony-structured barnacle inclusions to 6mm and probable bivalve. The presence of barnacle suggests the use of contemporary marine/inter-tidal shell species. The inner and outer surfaces of the rim show a series of light finger impressions indicating the separate attachment of the rim to the vessel body. Such construction marks are typical of Mid to Late Anglo-Saxon pottery in Kent (eg at Canterbury). Traces of sooting externally. Associated with two sherds of Ipswich ware in context 603 (the fill of pit F604, south of Structure 3).

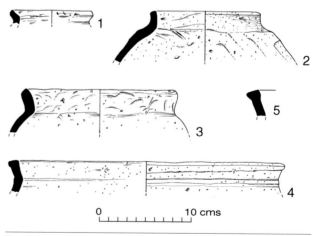

Fig 18. Post-Roman pottery. Anglo-Saxon wares, Nos 1–3; Early Medieval wares, Nos 4–5. Scale 1:4.

MLS5A Coarse sandy ware with sparse-moderate shell *c* AD 700–800. Sherds from a single thick-walled jar with external burnishing. Dark grey external surface, brownish-buff external margin, brownish-grey core with darker internal surface. Moderate medium-coarse rounded to sub-rounded quartz, commonly 0.5–1mm across with rare rounded grains to 2mm predominantly iron-stained and iron-coated, orange-red to dark brown, also clear. Moderate red-brown iron oxide, sized as quartz. Moderate fine mica. Rare coarse organic inclusions. Moderate coarse to very coarse shell inclusions up to 5mm, predominantly bony-structured barnacle with lesser amounts of bivalve, possibly including oyster, rare gastropod (?hydrobia), and rare forams to 0.2mm. All species indicative of the use of contemporary marine shell. Samples from Canterbury (in the Kent Fabric Reference Collection) are very similar and include specimens with orange-red iron-tinted quartz (though coarser) and barnacle.

MLS7A Ipswich ware: sandy *c* AD 720–850 (formerly CAT Fabric EMS6; Blinkhorn Group 1).Wheel-turned grey sandy ware produced at Ipswich, Suffolk. Wide, primarily coastal, distribution in eastern and southern England. The three sherds from Wainscott are all body sherds and appear to represent three separate vessels (not illustrated). One sherd comes from the fill (343) of pit F344 in the central pit group. The sherd, which is in a fresh condition, is from a smallish, globular, thick-walled jar with a very hard light grey fabric. It was associated with two joining sherds of organic-tempered ware. The two other sherds are from the same context (603) within a cess-pit (F604) lying 6m south of Structure 3. One sherd, in fairly fresh condition, is from a steep- almost straight-shouldered jar or wide-necked 'bottle' in a dark grey fabric. The other, which is abraded, is probably from the flattish basal area of a vessel with dark grey surfaces and a broad reddish-brown core. They were associated with three sherds of shelly ware (MLS5, including Fig 18.3).

Ipswich ware, in all its fabric varieties, is fairly common on the north Kent coast at Canterbury and Minster, Sheppey, most probably because of connections between the Kentish and East Anglian royal households. The main currency of the ware at Canterbury is thought to be from *c* AD 750 onwards (Macpherson-Grant 1995, 896). A major survey of the ware in England, including Kentish evidence, is forthcoming (Blinkhorn forthcoming; see also Blackmore 2001, 205–6). The nearest find-spots of Ipswich ware to Wainscott are just 3 miles away to the east at Black House, Gillingham, and 7 miles away to the south at White Horse Stone near Maidstone on the other side of the Medway valley (Paul Blinkhorn, pers comm). Other, more distant, north coast find-spots include Teynham, Deerton Street, near Faversham, and Seasalter near Whitstable. The forms commonly found in Kent are jars and spouted pitchers.

Early medieval wares (EM) *c* AD 1050–1225

EM1 Early medieval Canterbury sandy ware *c* AD 1050–1225. The commonest early medieval ware in east Kent; Wainscott lies at the very limits of its western distribution, although a

cooking pot in this fabric has been identified from nearby Eccles, near Aylesford. Typically brownish or brownish grey with abundant/profuse medium-coarse quartz sand temper. Represented here by a single small sherd (unstratified), part of an unglazed tubular spout from a spouted pitcher. Probably twelfth century. Identification as a Canterbury-type product is most likely. However, as the sherd is small and abraded an alternative identification cannot be ruled out

EM2 Shelly ware *c* AD 1050–1225. Pale brown to dark brownish-grey, sometimes (as Fig 18.4) with patchy orange-brown surfaces. Fairly soft. Little or no sand content. Moderate to abundant coarse shell, mostly voided or calcined making it almost impossible to discern shell species. Bivalve, however, appears likely. Abundant fine-medium red iron oxide (visible only in oxidised pieces). Very fine to fine mica is particularly evident as a matrix constituent of the Wainscott pieces. Large diameter hand-made jars/cooking pots with simple externally thickened/flat-topped rims (Figs 18.4–5), on general parallels most probably of eleventh- to mid twelfth-century date. It is not impossible that some pieces could be of Late Saxon date. Probably locally made. EM2-type sand-free shelly wares are found all over Kent but, as here, are the predominant early medieval type along the north-west coast of Kent.

EM3 Shelly-sandy wares *c* AD 1075–1225. Rare here. Apparently jars/cooking pots. A hard oxidised very sandy sherd is potentially of late twelfth- or early thirteenth-century date.

Dating implications

Overall the post-Roman pottery indicates two main periods of occupation at Wainscott: the first of Mid-Saxon date (*c* AD 750–850), and the second of early medieval date (*c* AD 1050–1150). There are much slighter indications of possible post-Roman activity on the site for a brief time shortly before and after these dates.

A few sherds of organic-tempered ware (EMS4) are potentially the earliest post-Roman ceramic type, though they are not closely datable. In general, organic-tempered wares are most typical of the sixth and seventh centuries. At Canterbury their main period of currency is thought to be *c* AD 550–725, but in more rural areas such as Wainscott they may have continued in production as late as *c* AD 800, by which time they were replaced by local shelly wares (or in the case of Canterbury, by sandy wares). Arguably, the organic-tempered sherds at Wainscott are datable to within the main period of Mid-Saxon occupation here, rather than representing a slightly earlier phase of activity. Of the seven sherds of the ware recovered only one sherd (context 279) does not occur either with Ipswich ware or, residually, with early medieval wares. This sherd occurs in isolation in a pit context (F280), one of a scatter of pits to the west of Anglo-Saxon Structure 4, some of which produced Mid-Saxon shelly wares thus indicating a date after *c* AD 750.

The main period of Mid-Saxon occupation *c* AD 750–850 is suggested by the presence of local shelly wares, of Mid-

Saxon character and technology, and sherds from three separate vessels in Ipswich ware. The latter type is securely dated to *c* AD 720–850, but is thought to have had its main currency at Canterbury after *c* AD 750. The start-date estimated for Mid-Saxon shelly wares at Canterbury largely relies on its association there with Ipswich ware and so is mainly taken to be from *c* AD 750, although some shelly fabric types could date from *c* AD 700 but were probably not common at this early date. Collectively, the evidence from Canterbury, Sheppey and Sandtun suggests a likely dating emphasis of *c* AD 775–850 for the Mid-Saxon activity at Wainscott.

There appears to be a complete absence of pottery types firmly datable to the Late Saxon period (*c* AD 850–1050), although some of the early medieval shelly wares could conceivably date to the very end of this period.

The second period of post-Roman occupation on the site is represented almost entirely by early medieval shelly wares (mainly sand-free EM2), the typology of which suggests a date of *c* AD 1050–1150. Almost half the total EM2 shelly ware assemblage came from a single context (242) within a field ditch (F3) on the west side of the site (Period 4). The complete absence of glazed London-type ware, common in north Kent from *c* AD 1140, also hints at an end to significant occupation by the middle of the twelfth century. One or two sherds (one unstratified, the other from well F300 (to the south of Structure 4, Period 3)) may date as late as *c* AD 1200, but may represent casual losses (field manuring?) after the main period of activity here.

Pottery sources, social status and conclusions

Apart from the Ipswich ware, all the Mid Anglo-Saxon pottery from the site could have been locally produced. Despite variations in hardness, texture and in the relative proportions of tempering agents employed there are underlying characteristics which unite the majority shell- or shell and sand-tempered wares into a closely related group irrespective of division into the fabric types discussed above. Three fabrics have distinctive reddish-brown iron-stained quartz (MLS4, MLS5 and MLS5A). The significance of this is not fully understood but iron-stained quartz is a characteristic of many pottery types produced from Wealden clays and sands (most of west Kent and Surrey). On the north coast of Kent, however, somewhat north of these deposits, pockets of iron-stained quartz sand occur in the Woolwich, Reading and Thanet Beds, outcropping close to Wainscott, and these rather than Wealden sources may have been exploited. The presence of contemporary marine rather than fossil shell also points to local manufacture. The Wainscott Mid-Saxon and early medieval shelly wares are also noticeably micaceous.

Some Mid-Saxon shell- and sand-tempered wares from Canterbury are remarkably similar both in terms of technology and petrology to some of the Wainscott wares (see above, MLS5A), though the source of these wares at Canterbury is presumably more local, though coastal.

The Wainscott assemblage, though small, highlights the predominance of shell-tempered wares along the north-west coast of Kent as early as the Mid-Saxon period, in contrast to the predominance of sand-tempered wares (MLS2) in the Canterbury and east Kent area – a distinction that persisted into the medieval period.

It is difficult to evaluate the social status of the Mid-Saxon settlement on the basis of such a small ceramic assemblage. The local wares appear to represent everyday cooking and storage vessels. The presence of three vessels in Ipswich ware, which might include spouted pitchers (for serving liquids) as well as cooking/storage vessels, is interesting but not necessarily that remarkable for a Mid-Saxon site on the north Kent coast. At the very least it indicates some level of involvement in regional coastal trade. On the other hand, the highest concentrations of Ipswich ware in north Kent are those associated with important royal and ecclesiastical sites such as Canterbury and the Mid-Saxon foundation at Minster in Sheppey. The presence of Ipswich ware at Wainscott, therefore, could conceivably be linked to the proximity of the nearby Mid-Saxon minster at Hoo St Werburgh, although the site of the latter has not yet been located and no Ipswich ware has been identified from the area. No Mid-Saxon Canterbury products were identified from Wainscott, nor any continental imports. In the absence of comparable Mid-Saxon assemblages from the area, the overall impression is of a fairly low-status domestic settlement, isolated but with some access to coastally traded goods.

Roman coins

Ian Anderson

A total of twenty-one coins were recovered from this site, all of Roman date (Table 9). With the exception of one coin of Hadrian, all are within a narrow date range of AD 260–90, the latest being two coins of Carausius, one with a mint-mark

Quantity	Date, type and context
1	Hadrian (AD 117–38). Dupondius, RIC 974 (378)
2	Gallienus (sole reign, AD 260–68). Antoninianus, RIC 267, (40). Antoninianus, RIC 321, (u/s)
2	Claudius II (AD 268–70). Antoninianus, RIC 105, (40). Antoninianus, RIC 149, (40)
3	Victorinus (AD 268–70). Antoninianus, RIC 43, (40). Antoninianus, RIC 114, (40), (95)
1	Tetricus I (AD 270–73). Antoninianus, as RIC 86, (40)
3	Tetricus II (AD 270–73). Antoninianus, RIC 248, (40). Antoninianus, as RIC 254, (40). Antoninianus, RIC 267, (1)
1	House of Tetricus (AD 270–73). Antoninianus, as RIC 111, (423)
6	Barbarous radiates (c AD 270–90). Obv VIC ..., rev Salus, (40). Obv Claudius II, rev uncertain, (339). Obv ... RICVSAV..., bust of Tetricus II, rev pontifical implements, (40). Obv Postumus? rev TEMP..., Felicitas, m.m.A/*, copied from Tacitus, cf RIC 63–65, (429). Obv and rev uncertain, (40), (429)
2	Carausius (AD 286–93). Antoninianus RIC 101, (40). Antoninianus, as RIC 121, (u/s)

Table 9. Roman coins.

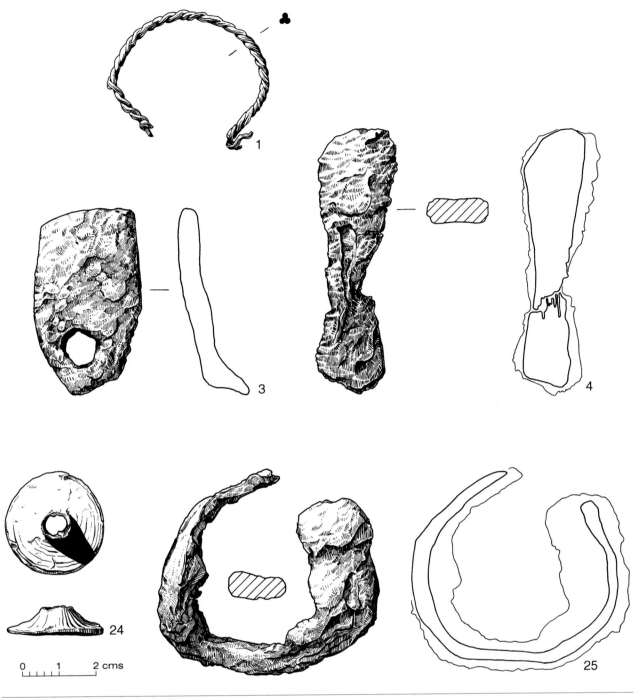

Fig 19. Roman small finds. Scale 1:1.

dated to AD 289–90, the other illegible. The group forms an unbroken sequence, suggesting the site was occupied for much of that period and was abandoned in or shortly after *c* AD 290, as indicated by the scarcity of Carausian coins. The presence of the Hadrian coin need not be anomalous as the contents of hoards have demonstrated that some first- and second-century coins did survive in circulation until the third century AD.

One particularly noteworthy coin is the barbarous radiate with the reverse copied from a coin of Tacitus, and coupled with what appears to be an obverse of Postumus. Most copies are based on Gallic and Central Empire issues up to AD 273,

and although copies based on later prototypes are known, they occur in much smaller numbers.

Roman small finds

Ian Riddler

Objects of Roman date include a bracelet, a hobnail, several fragments of querns, a copper alloy mount, a spindlewhorl, structural ironwork, metallurgical residues and several miscellaneous fragments of iron.

45

Dress accessories

Bracelet

A twin-strand copper alloy cable bracelet (1) came from a context of late Roman date. Its terminals have been removed and the object is a little distorted, but it can be assigned to Lankhills type A1, a common Roman form which is seen in some numbers from the third century onwards (Clarke 1979, 302; Crummy 1983, 38). Similar bracelets have come from late Roman contexts at Canterbury, Ickham and Dover (Bennett *et al* 1982, fig 90.42; Blockley *et al* 1995, 1028, nos 393–6; Bennett *et al* forthcoming; Philp 1981, 153 and fig 34.87).

1. An incomplete copper alloy twin-strand bracelet, for which the terminals have been cut away. Internal diameter: 38mm. FN 29, from (42) an occupation deposit adjacent to Enclosure 2, Period 2. Fig 19.

Hobnail

A single example of an iron hobnail came from a context of Roman date. Hobnails are very common finds on Roman sites in east Kent and examples have come from most sites of that date.

2. A complete iron hobnail, with a domed head. FN 711, from (277) the fill of pit F278, Period 2. Not illustrated.

Household items

Bucket-handle mounts

An iron strip with a rounded and perforated terminal (3) can be identified as a bucket-handle mount. Similar examples are known from Usk and *Verulamium*, amongst other sites (Manning 1985, 102; Frere 1972, fig 66.53–4; 1984, fig 41.76; Manning *et al* 1995, 202 and fig 54.23). A second strip of iron (4) tapers towards its centre and may have formed part of a longer version of the same object type. In addition to the mounts, part of an iron bucket handle (5) was also recovered, which recalls those from Well 1 at Dalton Parlours, as well as other sites (Manning 1985, 102–3; Wrathmell and Nicholson 1990, 197 and figs 116–7). All three objects are common Roman types.

3. A section of an iron bucket-handle mount, including a rounded terminal which is perforated. Length: 49mm. FN 167, from (345) an upper fill of the drainage system associated with Structure 1, Period 2. Fig 19.
4. A fragmentary iron strip which broadens at either end and has a flat, rectangular section. It is probably a part of a bucket-handle mount. FN 706, from (40) an upper fill of Enclosure 2, Period 2. Fig 19.
5. A curved iron rod of square section. A soil accretion towards one end may mask an additional fitting. The curvature of the rod and its section suggest that it is part of a bucket handle. Length: 160mm; width: 7mm; thickness: 6mm. FN 742, from (378) an upper fill of the drainage system associated with Structure 1, Period 2. Not illustrated.

Knife

Part of the blade for an iron knife (6) survives in poor condition. It is apparent, nonetheless, that the back is straight and that it is a relatively broad blade and these characteristics suggest that it is a knife of Roman date.

6. A part of the blade of an iron knife. The back of the blade is straight and it is relatively broad. FN 713, from (424) the fill of F302, Enclosure 2, Period 2. Not illustrated.

Querns

Ten fragments of basalt lava, weighing 0.785kg, came from a single context of Roman date. Most of the fragments are relatively small and none of their original dimensions can be reconstructed. In addition, four pieces of quern of the same material were retrieved from a context possibly of prehistoric date (Table 10).

Fragments of basalt lava querns first occur in late Iron Age contexts within Kent. Thereafter, they are common in Roman deposits. It has been considered that they were imported into southern England during the early Roman period, possibly for use by the army. In earlier texts it was noted that this importation was largely restricted to the early Roman period (Peacock 1980, 50; Lakin 1999, 330–1). Subsequently, however, it has become clear that basalt lava querns are much more widespread. Within Kent, they can be seen in late Roman contexts at Canterbury, Monkton and Ickham, and they occur at those sites throughout the Roman period (Blockley *et al* 1995, 1206, nos 1387–9; Riddler

No	Context	Feature	Context date	Stone type	Quantity	Weight (g)	Find no
7	269	Pit F270	Prehistoric?	Basalt lava	4	295	166
8	40	Enclosure 2	Roman	Basalt lava	1	560	164
9	40	Enclosure 2	Roman	Basalt lava	1	122	219
10	40	Enclosure 2	Roman	Basalt lava	8	103	482

Table 10. Late Iron Age and Roman quern fragments.

2008a; Bennett *et al* forthcoming). A similar situation may be postulated for the north of England, although in that region a stronger association between basalt lava querns and military sites may have persisted.

Fragments of basalt lava querns have been recovered from a series of Roman rural sites within Kent, including Fawkham, Great Hougham Court Farm, Monkton, Preston, Thamesmead and West Wickham.

Agricultural implements

Reaping hook

The central part of an iron implement (11) includes a part of the blade but has fractured at the junction with the socket. It can be identified, nonetheless, as a reaping hook of Manning's type 2 (Manning 1985, 55–7). Similar reaping hooks have been recovered from a number of Roman sites in east Kent, including Ickham and Monkton (Bennett *et al* forthcoming; Riddler 2008b, 215). Reaping hooks represent one of the most common types of agricultural implement, and they are widely distributed on Roman sites in southern England.

11   A fragmentary iron reaping hook, with a straight blade of rectangular section, which curves towards the tip. The end part of the blade is missing, as well as the junction with the socket. Length: 138mm; width: 12mm. FN 710, from (422), charcoal fill of drainage system associated with Structure 1, Period 2. Not illustrated.

Structural ironwork

The structural ironwork recovered from Roman contexts includes several joiners' dogs and a quantity of nails. One of the joiners' dogs (12) is relatively small and is fragmentary, as is often the case with this object type. It is similar to examples from *Verulamium* and Gorhambury (Frere 1984, fig 44.136; Neal *et al* 1990, fig 137.685). A second example (13) forms a more substantial staple, which is of square section across its central portion. It came from an Anglo-Saxon context. Both are common Roman types (Manning 1985, 131–2).

A total of forty-five iron nails were recovered from the excavations. Most of these came from contexts of Roman date, although several were from Anglo-Saxon or medieval contexts. All of the nails from Roman contexts are tabulated here (Table 11); those from later contexts are itemised in Table 14. Most of the Roman nails have shafts of square or rectangular section and flat, sometimes irregular heads, and they can be assigned to Manning's type 1 (Manning 1985, 184). Few are complete and no measurements have been taken of their lengths.

Joiners' dogs

12   A fragmentary iron object, which includes the vestiges of two arms of square section. It formed part of an iron joiners'

dog. FN 322, from (43) an occupation deposit adjacent to Enclosure 2, Period 2. Not illustrated.

13   A fragmentary iron object, which survives in poor condition. It is likely to be part of a heavy iron staple, of square section, for which the ends of the arms are now missing; length: 90mm; width: 15mm. FN 88, from (279) the fill of pit 280, Period 3. Not illustrated.

No	Context	Context date	Quantity	Weight (g)	Find No
14	10	Late Roman	1	47	716
15	40	Late Roman	2	16	215
16	40	Late Roman	23	607	717
17	42	Late Roman	1	13	718
18	90	Roman	1	18	720
19	345	Roman	3	32	724
20	370	Roman	1	19	725
21	422	Roman	1	6	727
22	429	Roman	1	16	729
23	443	Roman	1	24	730

Table 11. Iron nails from Roman contexts.

Miscellaneous items

Copper alloy mount

A circular pedestal mount (24) may possibly be a leaded bronze, given its weight. It has a hollow centre and has been sheared away at that point. It resembles a pedestal base from Lullingstone (Meates 1987, fig 28.133) but the original function of both items is unclear.

24   A fragmentary copper alloy pedestal mount with a hollow centre, across which the object has been broken. Diameter: 26mm; height: 7mm; weight: 6g. FN 213, from (40) an upper fill of Enclosure 2, Period 2. Fig 19.

Iron ring

An incomplete iron ring (25) can be compared with similar examples, of late Roman date, from Shakenoak (Brodribb *et al* 1968, 106 and fig 36.90; 1971, 122 and fig 51.115). Their original function is not clear; they may possibly have been used with horse harness.

25   An iron ring of rectangular section, one part of which is now fragmentary. Internal diameter: 50mm; width: 16mm. FN 218, from (40) an upper fill of Enclosure 2, Period 2. Fig 19.

Iron bindings

A fragment of iron binding (26) is unstratified but could well be of Roman date. Only the central part of the rectangular strip survives, and the original shape of the terminals cannot be reconstructed. A second fragment (27), from an Anglo-Saxon context, includes an iron ring within a perforation towards one end. Iron bindings were used on a variety of objects, including chests. A complete set of iron chest fittings of Roman date came from Milton Keynes (Musty and Manning 1977).

26 A section of a rectangular iron binding strip; Width: 37mm. FN 27, unstratified. Not illustrated.

27 A fragmentary section of rectangular iron binding strip, with a perforation towards one end, within which lies an incomplete iron ring. Width: 24mm. FN 708, from (412), fill of quarry 413, Period 3. Not illustrated.

Anglo-Saxon small finds

Ian Riddler

A wide variety of objects came from Anglo-Saxon contexts. Where these can be dated, they tend to belong to the earlier part of the Middle Saxon period, of the later seventh century and the eighth century. They include several pins, of bone and iron, sets of tweezers and keys, loomweights, fibre processing spikes and quern fragments. A re-used Roman spindlewhorl may be of early medieval date.

Middle Saxon objects remain a comparatively rare commodity in Kent and this small assemblage forms a useful addition to what is currently a small corpus. Middle Saxon rural sites, in particular, have emerged in recent years from Yorkshire and East Anglia, and the few sites of this date from Kent, including Cliffsend and Sandtun, as well as Wainscott, and Hassocks in Sussex, form a regional counterbalance for southern England (Milne and Richards 1992; Stamper and Croft 2000; Richards 1999; 2000; Butler 2000; Gardiner *et al* 2001).

Dress accessories

Bone pin

A fragmentary bone or antler object (28) can be identified as a Middle Saxon pin. It has a tapering section, which has been facetted by knife and is roughly finished at its apex. Pins with similar, vestigial heads are known from Ipswich (where they are defined as Type 4 pins) and Wharram Percy (Stamper and Croft 2000, fig 71.95). They form one of several types of small bone or antler pin of Middle Saxon date. The polished shaft of this example tends to corroborate its identification as a pin, rather than a peg.

28 A fragmentary bone or antler pin of circular cross-section which tapers from a lightly-expanded head. It is facetted by knife and is highly polished from use. FN 220, from (90) a drain cut associated with Structure 1, Period 2. Fig 20.

Iron pins

Single examples of iron pins (29 and 30) were recovered from two separate contexts. One of the pins (30) is fragmentary

and only a section of its shaft survives. The second pin (29), however, is complete, with a biconical head and a shaft that is lightly hipped towards the point. Two small rounded collars lie just below the head.

Iron pins have been found in a number of early Anglo-Saxon cemeteries, including Dover Buckland and Mill Hill, Deal (Evison 1987, 82–3; Parfitt and Brugmann 1997, 50–1). The presence of a biconical head on the complete example recalls pins of copper alloy from a slightly later date, however. Iron pins are commonly found in Middle Saxon settlements (Addyman and Hill 1969, 65). The biconical head form can be seen on copper alloy pins from Hamwic, Whitby, York and various other Middle Saxon sites (Hinton 1996, 25–8; Peers and Radford 1943, fig 14; Rogers 1993, fig 662). In general terms, the shapes of iron pins do not always mirror those of copper alloy or other materials precisely. This is the case at Shakenoak and at York, for example (Brodribb *et al* 1972, fig 52; Rogers 1993, 1367 and figs 662–6). In this particular instance, however, the head form is almost a type-fossil for the Middle Saxon period and it does suggest that this iron pin is of eighth- or ninth-century date. An iron pin with a biconical head came from Cottam, amidst an assemblage which does reflect Middle Saxon copper alloy pins more closely (Richards 1999, 77 and fig 50.39).

29 A complete iron pin, with a biconical head and a thin shaft, which is lightly hipped towards the point. Two small collars lie immediately below the head. Length: 60mm. FN 291, from (382) the upper fill of pit F383, Period 3. Not illustrated.

30 An iron shaft of circular section, tapering towards one end, forming part of an iron pin. FN 386, from (357) the fill of structural post-hole 358, Structure 4, Period 3. Not illustrated.

Personal possessions

Tweezers

A complete set of copper alloy tweezers (31) is of Anglo-Saxon date and belongs, in all probability, to the early part of the Middle Saxon period. They have a narrow end loop, which retains a circular wire suspension fitting. The arms flare from the loop and are edged by single bounding lines, which forms their only decoration.

These characteristics effectively distinguish this set of tweezers both from those of Roman date and from those belonging to the fifth or early sixth century, some of which resemble Roman types (Riha 1986, 33–8; Myres and Green 1973, 105). Sets with splayed arms can be seen in graves from the sixth century onwards, as with those from Edix Hill and Monkton, for example (Malim and Hines 1998, fig 3.43; Hawkes and Hogarth 1974, fig 9). The simple, linear edging pattern of the Wainscott set is paralleled at both Canterbury and Hamwic by tweezers for which the arms are rather more splayed, however (Blockley *et al* 1995,

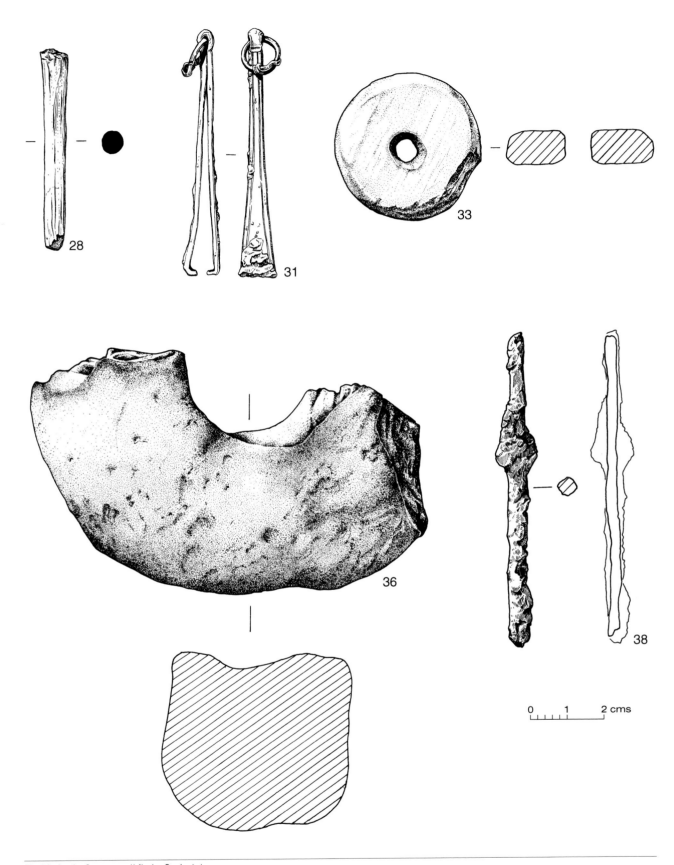

Fig 20. Anglo-Saxon small finds. Scale 1:1.

fig 443.469; Hinton 1996, fig 18.258/102). Lethbridge had previously noted that tweezers from a seventh-century grave at Shudy Camps 'are rather broader than those which we commonly find in the pagan graves' and by *c* AD 650 examples with this more exaggerated splay to the ends of the arms are commonly encountered (Lethbridge 1936, 2). The Wainscott set is more restrained in appearance and on that basis it should probably be assigned to the later sixth or seventh century.

Within early Anglo-Saxon graves, tweezers have usually been found in the inhumation graves of men, although examples do occur with some women (Evison 1987, 118; Scull 1992, 236; MacGregor and Bolick 1993, 221; Parfitt and Brugmann 1997, 77; Hinton 1996, 46; Malim and Hines 1998, 218). They are considered to have been used as cosmetic implements for plucking hair, although other functions are also possible, and the variety in both size and form suggests that not all were used for the same purpose (Rogers 1993, 1388; MacGregor and Bolick 1993, 221; Hinton 1996, 46).

31 A complete set of copper alloy tweezers, for which both arms are splayed from the narrow, rounded terminal loop. Each arm is decorated by single framing lines which run the length of the object from just below a transverse moulding beneath the terminal loop. A copper alloy suspension wire remains fastened to the terminal loop. Length: 65mm; width: 10mm. FN 325, from (527) the fill of pit F528, Period 3. Fig 20.

Set of iron keys

Part of a possible chatelaine arrangement with two iron keys (32) was recovered from a context thought to be of medieval date. It includes two iron rods with looped heads, which are joined to a circular iron ring. There is a clear resemblance with key sets of early and Middle Saxon date, although only a small portion of this example survives, and little can be said about its original components. Sets of iron keys attached to suspension loops are familiar, above all, from early Anglo-Saxon cemeteries, smaller examples like those here being used with casket locks (Evison 1987, 116–7). They have also been found, however, in Middle Saxon contexts, as with a chatelaine arrangement at York, for which Rogers has argued on typological grounds that they were not used after the seventh century (Rogers 1993, 1425–8). Elements of iron keys and girdle hangers have, however, been found subsequently in Middle Saxon contexts (Whytehead *et al* 1989, 124; Richards 1999, 79).

32 A fragment of a chatelaine arrangement, with two iron rods with looped heads, which are joined to a central circular iron ring. The iron rods are fragmentary and may originally have formed part of keys or other implements. FN 86, from (268) a buried soil associated with ditches F3, F21 and F308, Period 4. Not illustrated.

Textile manufacturing implements

Spindlewhorl

A near-complete discoidal spindlewhorl (33) has been expertly produced from a re-used sherd of grey ware. Spindlewhorls manufactured from re-used ceramics are generally the most common to be found in Roman contexts, as recent publications indicate (Bishop 1996, 32–3; Wilmott *et al* 1997, 288–9; Manning *et al* 1995, 251–4). Within Kent, they can be seen on almost all sites of Roman date, including Canterbury, Lullingstone, Maidstone and Ickham (Blockley *et al* 1995, 1170; Meates 1987, 59 and fig 21.39–47; Riddler 1999, 110 and fig 11.10; Bennett *et al* forthcoming). They are found in late Iron Age contexts and occur also throughout the Roman period.

This example is unusual, however, for the care that has been taken to round and smooth its edges and surfaces. Most of the spindlewhorls of this type from Roman contexts are roughly finished (Blockley *et al* 1995, 1170). One of the Roman spindlewhorls from Dolland's Moor, however, had also been ground and smoothed (Rady forthcoming), as also had several of the examples from Birdoswald (Wilmott *et al* 1997, figs 201.117 and 208.148). Mann has drawn attention to the careful finishing on early medieval ceramic spindlewhorls from Lincoln that also utilise Roman ceramics (Mann 1982, 22). They are relatively common finds from late Saxon and early medieval contexts, and examples are known also from Northampton, St Neots, Thetford, Winchester and York (Williams 1979, 288, SW20–37; Addyman 1973, fig 18.4; Rogerson and Dallas 1984, 117 and fig 152; Biddle 1990, 225; Walton Rogers 1997, 1735). Spindlewhorls made from re-used pot sherds found at Canterbury were thought to be entirely of Roman date, although some were retrieved from post-Roman contexts (Blockley *et al* 1995, 1170). The Wainscott example came from an early medieval context, and it may well have been fashioned at that time.

33 An incomplete ceramic spindlewhorl, produced from a sherd of a Roman grey ware vessel. The edge has been neatly rounded and the object is perforated, a little off centre, with a hole that is cylindrical in profile. Weight: 16g; diameter: 38mm; thickness: 8mm; perforation diameter: 7mm. FN 85, from (242) the fill of ditch F3, Period 4. Fig 20.

Loomweights

Five fragments, stemming from three loomweights, were recovered from three separate contexts of Anglo-Saxon date. All three loomweights were manufactured from the same, relatively clean brickearth fabric, with sparse inclusions of white and grey quartz. In two cases (34 and 35) the fragments are too small to be able to determine the type of loomweight from which they derive. Sufficient survives of the third example (36), however, to enable it to be identified as of intermediate type. It was originally *c* 125mm in diameter, with a thickness of 50mm and an original weight of *c* 500g.

No	Context	Context date	Quantity	Weight (g)	Find No
40	0	unstratified	2	60	715
41	82	Medieval	3	38	719
42	114	Anglo-Saxon or early medieval	1	6	721
43	285	Anglo-Saxon	1	3	722
44	339	Anglo-Saxon	2	58	723
45	412	Anglo-Saxon	1	9	726

Table 12. Post-Roman basalt lava quern fragments.

No	Context	Context date	Quantity	Weight (g)	Find No
46	140		2	1150	251
47	218		2	20	428
48	307		2	3	203
49	343	Anglo-Saxon	1	800	133
50	443		1	375	612
51	607		1	635	475

Table 13. Metallurgical residues.

No	Context	Context date	Quantity	Weight (g)	Find No
52	82	Medieval	3	38	719
53	114	Anglo-Saxon or early medieval	1	6	721
54	285	Anglo-Saxon	1	3	722
55	339	Anglo-Saxon	2	58	723
56	412	Anglo-Saxon	1	9	726

Table 14. Iron nails from post-Roman contexts.

The estimated weight of this example equates well with contemporary loomweights from London, which range from 380–700g, although most are centred on 450–600g.

Intermediate loomweights can be distinguished from annular and bun-shaped forms on the basis of the size of the central aperture. With intermediate examples, as here, the diameter of the aperture is broadly equivalent to the thickness of the clay ring (Cowie *et al* 1988, 111). This type of loomweight is essentially of Middle Saxon date, with most examples belonging to the eighth and ninth centuries. They are commonly seen at this time, both in urban and rural contexts, although few examples have been published as yet, from Kent. The Kent sample is largely limited to loomweights from Canterbury (Blockley *et al* 1995, 1173, nos 1215–6 and 1218).

34   Three small fragments from a ceramic loomweight, fired to an orange colour with a reduced core. The fabric is sandy, with sparse inclusions of white and grey quartz. Weight: 45g. FN 89, from (279) the fill of pit 280, Period 3. Not illustrated.

35   A small fragment of a ceramic loomweight. It has been fired to a buff to grey colour with a grey core, in a sandy fabric with sparse inclusions of grey and white quartz. Weight: 71g. FN 387, from (527) the fill of pit F528, Period 3. Not illustrated.

36   A fragment from a ceramic loomweight of intermediate type. Approximately 37.5 per cent of the loomweight survives. It has been fired to an orange to red colour, in a sandy fabric with few inclusions, aside from occasional fragments of white and grey quartz. There is a trace of a possible cord mark on one side. Weight: 189g; estimated original weight: 506g; thickness: 50mm; diameter: 130mm. FN 212, from (361) the fill of ditch F308, Period 4. Fig 20.

Fibre processing spikes

Three fibre processing spikes (37, 38 and 39) were recovered from separate contexts. Each example has a shaft of circular section that tapers to a point and is lightly curved. They conform to examples of Anglo-Saxon date rather than medieval spikes, which were generally longer (Walton Rogers 1997, 1727–30). It is not possible to determine whether they were secured into a wooden or an iron frame and, accordingly, they are described as fibre processing spikes. They may have formed part of one or more wool-combs, or flax heckles, object types which are relatively common in Middle Saxon and later contexts.

Two of the examples come from Anglo-Saxon or medieval contexts, whilst the third, fragmentary spike (39) was recovered from a Roman deposit. Similar spikes were used

No	Material	Object	Quantity	Context	Object dating	Find no
28	bone or antler	pin	1	90	Middle Saxon	220
34	ceramic	loomweight	1	279	Anglo-Saxon	89
35	ceramic	loomweight	1	527	Anglo-Saxon	387
36	ceramic	loomweight	1	361	Middle Saxon	212
33	ceramic	spindlewhorl	1	242	early medieval	85
1	copper alloy	bracelet	1	42	Late Roman	29
24	copper alloy	pedestal mount	1	40	Roman	213
31	copper alloy	tweezers	1	527	Middle Saxon	325
26	iron	binding strip	1	unstratified	Roman?	27
27	iron	binding strip	1	412	Roman?	708
5	iron	bucket handle	1	378	Roman	742
3	iron	bucket handle mount	1	345	Roman	167
4	iron	bucket handle mount	1	40	Late Roman	706
39	iron	fibre processing spike	1	422	Roman	709
37	iron	fibre processing spike	1	335	Anglo-Saxon	385
38	iron	fibre processing spike	1	114	Anglo-Saxon	83
2	iron	hobnail	1	277	Roman	711
12	iron	joiner's dog	1	43	Roman	322
13	iron	joiner's dog	1	279	Roman	88
6	iron	knife	1	424	Roman	713
46	iron	metallurgical residue	2	140	Anglo-Saxon	251
47	iron	metallurgical residue	2	218	Anglo-Saxon	428
48	iron	metallurgical residue	2	307	Anglo-Saxon	203
49	iron	metallurgical residue	1	343	Anglo-Saxon	133
50	iron	metallurgical residue	1	443	Anglo-Saxon	612
51	iron	metallurgical residue	1	607	Anglo-Saxon	475
14	iron	nail	1	10	Roman	716
15	iron	nail	1	40	Roman	215
16	iron	nail	1	40	Roman	717
17	iron	nail	1	42	Roman	718
18	iron	nail	1	90	Roman	720
19	iron	nail	1	345	Roman	724
20	iron	nail	1	370	Roman	725
21	iron	nail	1	422	Roman	727
22	iron	nail	1	429	Roman	729
23	iron	nail	1	443	Roman	730
52	iron	nail	3	82	Anglo-Saxon	719
53	iron	nail	1	114	Anglo-Saxon	721
54	iron	nail	1	285	Anglo-Saxon	722
55	iron	nail	2	339	Anglo-Saxon	723
56	iron	nail	1	412	Anglo-Saxon	726
29	iron	pin	1	382	Middle Saxon	291
30	iron	pin	1	357	Middle Saxon?	386
11	iron	reaping hook	1	422	Roman	710
25	iron	ring	1	40	Roman	218
32	iron	set of keys	1	268	Middle Saxon	86
7	stone	quern	4	269	Roman	166
8	stone	quern	1	40	Roman	164
9	stone	quern	1	40	Roman	219
10	stone	quern	8	40	Roman	482
40	stone	quern	2	0	Roman or Anglo-Saxon	715
41	stone	quern	3	82	Anglo-Saxon	719
42	stone	quern	1	114	Anglo-Saxon	721
43	stone	quern	1	285	Anglo-Saxon	722
44	stone	quern	2	339	Anglo-Saxon	723
45	stone	quern	1	412	Anglo-Saxon	726

Table 15. Small finds.

during the Roman period and examples have been retrieved from Ickham, near Canterbury (Bennett *et al* forthcoming). This example may, therefore, be of Roman date.

37 A complete iron spike from a wool-comb or flax heckle. The spike is circular in section and a slight widening of the profile below the head may indicate the junction with its wooden or iron frame. Length: 106mm. FN 385, from (335) the fill of cut feature 336, Period 3. Not illustrated.

38 An incomplete iron spike from a wool-comb or flax heckle. The spike is circular to oval in section and tapers slightly over the surviving length. Both ends are now missing and the spike has been bent over at some point in antiquity. FN 83, from (114) the fill of ditch F115, adjacent to Structure 4, Period 3. Fig 20.

39 The shaft of an iron fibre processing spike, which is lightly curved towards its end. FN 709, from (422) the charcoal fill of drainage system associated with Structure 1, Period 2.

Household implements

Querns

Eight small fragments of basalt lava querns, weighing 114g, were recovered from five separate contexts of Anglo-Saxon or early medieval date. A further two fragments were unstratified (Table 12).

By the late Roman period basalt lava querns were being produced in a circular, discoidal shape for both upper and lower stones, and this essential form was retained during the Anglo-Saxon period. Basalt lava querns occur again in Kent from the seventh century onwards, and continue in use up to and beyond the Norman Conquest. The fragments listed in Table 12 could be of Roman or Anglo-Saxon origin, and they are too small to retain any diagnostic characteristics.

Craftworking implements and waste materials

Metallurgical waste

Though no tools for craftworking could be identified within the finds assemblage, a small quantity of ferrous metalworking residues, indicates that iron was being worked in the vicinity. All of the residues come from contexts of Anglo-Saxon or medieval date (Table 13).

Structural ironwork

Nails

Most of the nails from the site came from Roman contexts, as noted above. Several were also retrieved, however, from Anglo-Saxon and medieval contexts (Table 14).

Roman brick and tile

Louise Harrison

Just over half a tonne of Roman brick and tile was recovered from the excavations. The assemblage is both unusual and important because a large proportion of the material consists of 'waster' tiles, being overfired and distorted in shape, suggesting the presence of a tile kiln nearby. Additionally, a large quantity of the material has characteristics such as trimming, clear flange types and cutaways (in the case of *tegulae*), paw-print and hobnail impressions, signature marks and measurable dimensions.

The bulk of the material came from the backfill of Structure 1. Its composition has been analysed in relation to the stratigraphy in an attempt to ascertain whether any of the brick or tile came from the structure and to clarify the nature of its collapse.

The material

A total quantity of 1,699 complete and fragmented bricks and tiles weighing 549.345kg was retrieved from the excavation and forms the basis of this report. The composition of the assemblage by tile type is presented in Table 16.

The fabrics were identified using a x10 microscope. The following fabric descriptions are based on the CAT Roman brick and tile fabric typology (in preparation). All are red/orange in colour unless otherwise stated.

Form	Quantity	Quantity (%)	Weight (kg)	Weight (%)
Brick	221	13.00	156.95	28.60
Flue tile	10	0.60	1.75	0.30
Imbrex	65	3.80	7.94	1.40
Tegulae body fragments	729	42.90	119.02	21.70
Tegula	674	39.70	263.35	48.00
Totals	1699	100.00	549.00	100.00

Table 16. Quantities and weights of tile types present.

Fabric 1

This is a fine sandy fabric with very few large quartz grains; occasional calcareous inclusions are sometimes present.

The fabric is very similar to tile excavated from two kiln sites in Canterbury situated at Whitehall Gardens and St Stephen's (Jenkins 1956; 1960). However, considering the location the material is much more likely to have been produced locally.

Fabric 2

This is a very fine fabric which is not sandy. It contains few, if any inclusions in the matrix. Very occasionally, calcareous inclusions are visible. This fabric may be a non-sandy variant of fabric 1.

Fabric 5

This fabric has a large quantity of iron oxide and a scatter of small (>0.5mm) quartz grains.

Fabric 8

The most distinctive feature of this fabric is its colour, which varies from white and cream to yellow or pale orange. Additionally, there is a scatter of (usually small) clear, 'rose' and white coloured quartz grains (up to 0.5mm) and occasionally red clay pellets or lenses are visible. The sanding on the back of these tiles consists of 'rose' coloured quartz. This fabric was produced in Eccles, north-west Kent from around AD 50–60 to the early second century AD (Betts 1992).

Fabric 10

This is a fine sandy fabric with characteristic common black oxides appearing abundantly in the matrix; occasional red clay inclusions are also present.

A similar fabric has been identified in London as coming from Radlett in Hertfordshire, though the London examples are sandier and have a larger quantity of black oxide inclusions (Ian Betts, pers comm).

Fabric 11

This fine, slightly sandy fabric is pale orange/red in colour. Its characteristic feature is cream coloured 'swirls' or lenses (silty inclusions) appearing commonly in the matrix. Additionally, a scatter of small quartz grains (0.5mm) is also present. This fabric was produced in London or nearby and is dated (in London) to *c* AD 120 (Ian Betts, pers comm).

It is very likely that many of the examples classified as fabric 1 could in fact be a variant of fabric 10. This is because it is possible that the overfiring process in some of the tiles has removed (or leached out) the black inclusions (iron oxides) that are so characteristic of fabric 10 (Ian Betts, pers comm).

Table 17 shows how many tiles were present in each fabric type; fabric 10 and fabric 1 were most common, representing 63.4 per cent and 35.4 per cent of the assemblage respectively by quantity. The remaining fabric types were very poorly represented (under 1.1 per cent of the assemblage by quantity), consisting of small, abraded, probably residual fragments of brick and tile.

Table 18 again indicates that fabric 10 and 1 were the most commonly represented fabric types. It also shows that all tile types (except flue tile which was poorly represented in the assemblage overall) were commonly found in both fabric 10 and fabric 1.

Fabric type	Quantity	Quantity (%)	Weight (kg)	Weight (%)
1	602	35.43	161.03	29.31
2	1	0.06	0.20	0.04
5	3	0.18	0.44	0.08
8	9	0.53	0.45	0.08
10	1078	63.45	386.21	70.30
22	1	0.06	0.13	0.02
1/2	2	0.12	0.58	0.11
1/3	1	0.06	0.10	0.02
1/5	2	0.12	0.21	0.04
Totals	1699	100.00	549.35	100.00

Table 17. Quantities of fabric types.

Overfired and distorted tiles

One of the most distinguishing features of the material from Wainscott was the high proportion of tiles that were overfired and distorted in shape, or were knife trimmed on their underside (to achieve a smooth base) or showed evidence of both (Table 19). This overfiring and trimming is thought to be a characteristic of tile that was produced at Wainscott and was therefore analysed in greater detail.

In total, 141 tiles (43.600kg) were overfired (8.2 per cent by quantity), 661 tiles (272.980kg) were trimmed (38.9 per cent by quantity), and 153 tiles (78.660kg) showed evidence of both (9 per cent by quantity).

The brick and tile was also considered by fabric to establish how many of each fabric were overfired, trimmed or showed evidence of both (Table 20). The table shows that a larger quantity of tiles consisting of fabric 1 showed evidence of overfiring than those consisting of fabric 10. Again, this suggests that it is possible that the overfiring process in some of the tiles has removed (or leached out) the black inclusions (iron oxides) that are so characteristic of fabric 10.

Brick

Many of the fragmentary bricks only had a thickness measurement, which was often difficult to ascertain due to the many overfired and distorted examples present in the assemblage. These brick fragments had thicknesses varying from 20–70mm. Because a wide range of different brick types share the same thickness, it is often difficult to positively identify them to type. The range in thickness suggests that the fragments are parts of *bessalis*, *pedalis*, *lydion* and possibly *sesquipidalis* bricks. A small number of bricks were more complete and had dimensions other than thickness, allowing them to be more accurately identified (Table 21).

The size of these bricks is smaller than the average brick (Brodribb 1987, 34–41). Bricks tended to decrease in size throughout the Roman period, suggesting that these bricks date from the mid second to the early third century (Ian Betts, pers comm). This would seem to complement the date of the *tegulae* discussed below.

Fabric	1	2	5	8	10	22	1/2	1/3	1/5
Brick	111	0	0	0	110	0	0	0	0
Flue tile	1	0	0	0	8	1	0	0	0
Imbrex	34	0	0	0	31	0	0	0	0
Tegula	137	0	0	3	534	0	0	0	0
Tegula body fragments	319	1	3	6	395	0	2	1	2

Table 18. Fabric distribution by tile type.

	Brick Flue		*Tegula* body fragments		Imbrex		*Tegula*	
	No	Weight (kg)	No	Weight (kg)	No	Weight (kg)	No	Weight (kg)
Overfired and distorted	35	26.02	83	11.80	5	0.38	18	5.41
Trimmed	54	39.03	212	52.93			395	181.02
Both	49	38.78	41	11.74			63	28.14

Table 19. Numbers of tiles (by type) overfired, trimmed or both.

		Brick	*Tegulae* body fragments	Imbrex	*Tegula*
Fabric 1	overfired	29	63	3	15
	trimmed	10	60	0	47
	overfired and trimmed	42	31	0	40
Fabric 1/5	overfired	0	1	0	0
Fabric 5	trimmed	0	2	0	0
Fabric 10	overfired	6	19	2	3
	trimmed	45	150	0	348
	overfired and trimmed	7	10	0	23

Table 20. Numbers of tiles (by tile and fabric type) overfired, trimmed or both.

Brick type	Length mm	Width mm	Thickness mm	Comments
Bessalis	?	198	25/30	overfired and distorted Fabric 1
Bessalis	?	193	25	Fabric 10
Lydion	375	265	30	Signature mark Type 2, Fabric 10
Lydion	365	269/267	38/35	Signature mark Type 2, Fabric 10
Lydion	375/371	?	32/31	Signature mark Type 2, Fabric 10
Lydion	?	234	31	Fabric 10
Lydion	?	234	33	Fabric 10

Table 21. Available dimensions of complete or virtually complete bricks.

Flue tile

Flue tile was very poorly represented in the assemblage from Wainscott (0.6 per cent by quantity). They have been identified by type according to the CAT typology. The following keying types were present:

Type 8b: flue fragment combed with a rough lattice pattern. Teeth: 3, width of stroke: 18mm.

Type 5b: flue fragment combed with a diagonal cross with vertical stroke down the centre of the tile, it also has a square or rectangular cutaway 65/70mm from base/top. Teeth: 9, width of stroke: 47mm.

Type 14?: flue fragment combed with a diagonal cross. Teeth: 8, width of stroke: 31mm. Fig 21.1.

Type 23: flue corner fragment with a diagonal cross with vertical and horizontal border. Teeth: 7, width of stroke: 40mm. Fig 21.2.

Roofing tile

Imbrices

The *imbrices* were poorly represented in the assemblage from Wainscott (3.8 per cent by quantity). All were fragmentary and had no dimensions or very few characteristic features (overfiring, trimming or markings) other than thickness which varied from 11–20mm.

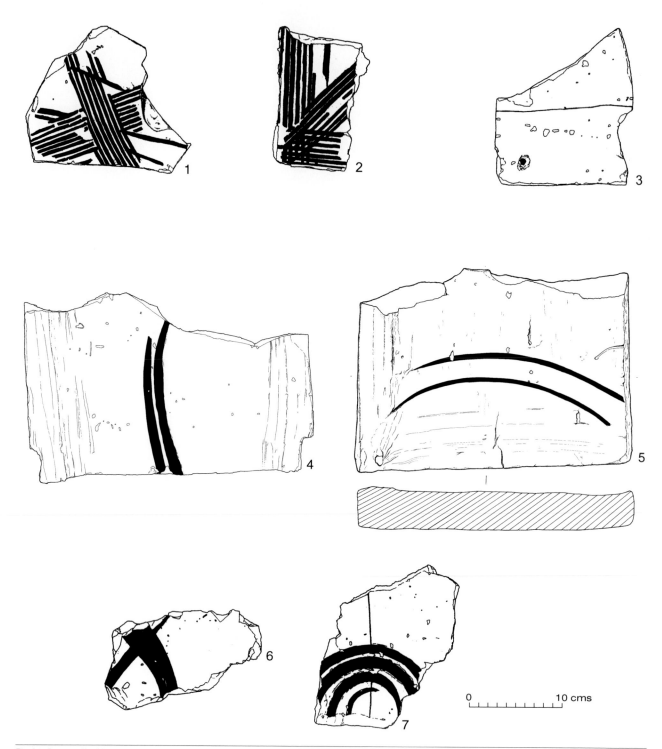

Fig 21. Roman tile. No 1, flue tile type 14?; No 2, flue tile type 23; No 3, tegula with nail hole; Nos 4–5, signature mark type 2; No 6, signature mark type 36; No 7, signature type 22. Scale 1:4.

Tegulae

Tegulae represented 39.7 per cent of the assemblage by quantity. Only five *tegulae* were complete enough to show dimensions other than thickness; from these it can be deduced that the length varied from 370 to 387mm, and the width varied from 283 to 312mm. Tiles tended to decrease in size throughout the Roman period; given these dimensions, these tiles may be roughly dated to the mid second to the early third

century (Ian Betts, pers comm). Additionally, there is one nail-hole present that was made before the tile was fired, this also a feature of tile produced from the mid second century onwards (Fig 21.3; Ian Betts, pers comm).

The *tegulae* were recorded by fabric, flange and (upper and lower) cutaway type where clear enough to do so. Table 22 shows the most commonly represented and positively identified flange types by fabric. The details of the less common and unclear flange types can be found in the site

Fabric	Flange type	Quantity
1	12	14
1	13	72
10	12	50
10	13	286
10	1	19
10	2	13

Table 22. Common flange types by fabric.

Fabric	Tile type	Signature mark	Quantity
1	Brick	1	1
1	Brick	2	8
1	Brick	18	1
1	*Tegula*	2	7
1	*Tegula* body fragments	2	23
2	*Tegula* body fragments	2	1
10	Brick	1	1
10	Brick	2	14
10	*Tegula*	1	1
10	*Tegula*	2	36
10	*Tegula*	18	2
10	*Tegula* body fragments	1	2
10	*Tegula* body fragments	2	63
10	*Tegula* body fragments	5	2
10	*Tegula* body fragments	18	1
10	*Tegula* body fragments	24	2
10	*Tegula* body fragments	new	1

Table 24. Numbers of each signature mark type present in each tile type (by fabric).

Impression type	Tile types	Quantity
Cat/kitten	*Tegula*, *tegula* body fragments	5
Dog	Brick, *tegula*, *tegula* body fragments	110
Finger	Brick, *tegula*, *tegula* body fragments	15
Goat	*Tegula*, *tegula* body fragments	4
Graffito	Brick, *tegula* body fragments	2
Hob nail shoe	Brick, *tegula*, *tegula* body fragments	25
Textile	*Tegula* body fragments	1

Table 25. Types of impressions found in the Wainscott assemblage.

archive. The table clearly shows that flange types 13 and to a lesser extent flange type 12 were the most common.

The lower cutaways of *tegulae* with positively identifiable flange types were also studied (Table 23) and it can be seen that lower cutaway type 'e' was the most common. It was also apparent that certain lower cutaway types appeared to be used with particular flange types. The eighty-four fragments of *tegulae* (fabrics 1 and 10) which had flange type 13 also had lower cutaway type 'e'. Of the eighty-one examples of overfired *tegulae* (fabrics 1 and 10), fifty-eight pieces had flange type 13; seventeen of these also had lower cutaway type 'e'. The surviving complete upper cutaways of flange 13 varied in length from 15 to 47mm.

Tile that had no flanges or cutaways but had a thickness similar to *tegulae* have been classed as *tegulae* body fragments. These represent 42.9 per cent of the assemblage and range in thickness from 10 to 70mm. They also share the same characteristics such as overfiring and trimming as *tegulae*.

Lower cutaway	Quantity
A	2
B	5
C	28
D	96

Table 23. Quantities of lower cutaways.

Brick and tile with signature marks

Overall, 166 brick and tile fragments (9.8 per cent by quantity) bore signature marks on their surfaces; only the most clear and complete examples have been illustrated. Again the signature mark types (for example, type 2; Figs 21.4 and 21.5) are based on the CAT typology. Table 24 clearly shows that signature mark type 2 was the most commonly represented in each tile type. The other signature marks present in the assemblage often only consisted of one or two examples (Figs 21.6 and 21.7).

Human and animal impressions

Another characteristic of the Wainscott material was the large quantity of brick and tile that had animal and human impressions on their surfaces. These totalled 162 fragments (9.5 per cent by quantity) and consisted of dog and cat paw-

prints, goat/sheep hoof-prints, hobnail shoe impressions and finger-prints (Table 25). There were also two examples of graffiti, one resembling a building (Fig 22.8), the other appearing as rough scratching on the surface of a brick.

The most common impressions were dog paw-prints and consisted of predominantly medium-sized paw-prints, probably from a dog roughly the size of an adult Labrador. There are many examples, some showing three or four paw prints on one tile where a dog has walked across it. Additionally, some show where a dog has probably slipped on a tile. One particular example has a paw-print and an impression that appears to be a stone. It is tempting to think that the stone was thrown at the dog to get it off the tiles.

There was also an unusually large quantity of hobnail shoe impressions present in the assemblage (1.4 per cent by quantity; Figs 22.9 and 22.10). It appears that the people living and working in the area were careless and often walked over unfired tiles left in the open to dry off.

Burnt brick and tile

Much of the material showed signs of burning; this represented 60 per cent of the assemblage by quantity. The details of all

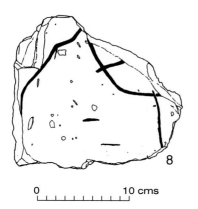  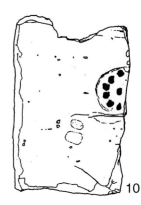

Fig 22. Roman tile. No 8, graffiti; Nos 9 and 10, hobnail impressions. Scale 1:4.

these tiles are shown on Table 26. Approximately sixty-two fragments weighing 36.460kg (3.6 per cent by quantity) was from the east flue wall of Structure 1 (context 85).

Form	Quantity	Weight (kg)
Brick	23	30.06
Imbrex	2	0.175
Tegulae body fragments	32	79.65(?)
Tegula	61	24.626

Table 26. Number of burnt tiles.

Stratigraphic information

One objective for studying this corpus of brick and tile was to establish whether any of the layers of tile represented the collapse of the upper fabric of Structure 1.

The most important group of tile in terms of its stratigraphy and what can be established by its presence is from the complicated backfill sequence within the walls of Structure 1 (context numbers 94, 96, 370, 393, 427, 428, 438, 439, 442 and 459). This brick and tile has been closely

Tile type	Quantity	Weight (kg)	Overfired
Brick	108	79.475	48 (35.57 kg)
Flue tile	1	0.54	
Imbrex	6	1.33	1 (0.105 kg)
Tegulae body fragments	192	45.07	50 (12.405 kg)
Tegula	292	133.34	50 (23.04 kg)

Table 27. Brick and tile from the infilling of Structure 1.

Form	Quantity	Weight (kg)	Overfired
Brick	9	16.22	
Tegulae body fragments	67	17.065	3 (0.380 kg)
Tegula	117	58.35	1 (0.315 kg)

Table 28. Brick and tile from the flue wall of Structure 1.

analysed to establish whether the tile was derived from the structure's upper fabric or was dumped there after the building was demolished (Table 27).

The table shows that this group of tile consists of a mixture of roofing tile, brick and wasters. Because of the variety of tile types present (and especially the considerable quantity of wasters), this would indicate that the group of tile was probably from a dumped deposit and not from the structure's upper fabric. It consisted of the two main fabrics present in the assemblage, fabric 1 (210 fragments, 79.820kg) and fabric 10 (389 fragments, 179.740kg).

The brick and tile that was used to form the flue wall (85) was also analysed to ascertain whether there was a difference between the tile used in construction and the tile retrieved from the dumped deposits. Table 28 shows that there was only a very small quantity of overfired tiles (2 per cent by quantity) used within the flue wall. This would seem likely because it would have been unusual for overfired and distorted tiles to have been used in the construction of the structure. It contained fragments in fabric 1 (thirty-seven fragments, 6.255kg) and fabric 10 (156 fragments, 85.380kg).

It is not known whether the tile used to form the structure and the tile retrieved from the infill of the structure consisted of tile produced at one or more kilns. All that can be said is that fabric 10 and to a lesser extent fabric 1 were the most commonly represented within both of these phases and were most likely to have been products of the same kiln (see fabric descriptions).

Conclusion

The corpus of brick and tile discussed above is important because it is a large sample of material, (46.6 per cent by quantity), most of which was used to form Structure 1 or was from the dumped deposits within it. Many of these were 'waster tiles' showing evidence of overfiring and distortion in their size and shape. The large quantity of wasters suggests that although no kiln was found, it is very likely that one was situated nearby and producing ceramic building material, mainly brick, *tegulae* and probably *imbrices*.

The brick and tile consisted of two main fabrics (fabrics 1 and 10). A larger quantity of fabric 1 showed evidence of overfiring than those consisting of fabric 10. These two fabrics were similar except that fabric 10 had black oxides while fabric 1 did not. Considering the large quantity of wasters it is likely that overfiring removed (leached out) the black oxides that are so characteristic of fabric 10 (*see* p 54). These two fabrics are most likely to have been the typical clay types used to manufacture the brick and tile produced at Wainscott.

The material shared a number of common characteristics which has allowed a basic typology for tile produced at Wainscott to be created. A large quantity of the *tegulae* and the brick was trimmed on the underside. The most common flange type used (in the case of the *tegulae*) was flange type 13 and to a lesser extent type 12. The most common lower cutaway type employed was cutaway type 'e'. Additionally, considering the large quantity of tiles, only a small number of different signature marks were present indicating only a few people being involved in the tile making operation. The most common signature mark was type 2, a two-grooved semi-circle.

The presence of the large number of animal and human impressions suggests that the tile may have been made close to or within a smallholding housing these animals. The smaller than average size of the bricks and tiles suggests that they date from the mid second to the early third century.

The quality of the material with many overfired or badly made, the large quantity of animal and human impressions and the lack of a wide variety of different signature marks seems to suggest that the tile at Wainscott was produced here on a short term, temporary and probably amateur basis.

4

Palaeoenvironmental evidence

Animal bone

Robin Bendrey

Hand-excavation recovered 746 fragments of bone weighing 9619 grams, of which 37.5 per cent by number, and 83.1 per cent by weight, have been identified. This material derived from contexts dating to Periods 2, 3 and 4; that from Period 4 has been further divided into three sub-periods (4a, 4b and 4c; Table 29). The animal bones are fairly well preserved, but the condition of preservation does vary. Carnivore gnawing damage is only recorded on 2.7 per cent of the total assemblage (Table 30).

Methodology

The animal bones were identified with the aid of a comparative osteological reference collection, and a number of publications (Baxter 1998; Eisenmann 1986; Schmid 1972); and recorded using the diagnostic zones of Dobney and Reilly (1988). Fragments not identified to species were awarded an animal-size category; otherwise were labelled indeterminate. The criteria of Boessneck (1969) and Payne (1985) have been used to differentiate between the bones of sheep and goat (Table 29). Bones identified to sheep/goat are considered within the taxon sheep in the report and Tables 30–34. Cattle, pig and sheep mandibular toothwear data have been recorded following Grant (1982). Measurements have been taken following von den Driesch (1976), except where indicated. The assemblage is quantified by number of fragments (NISP), minimum number of elements (MNE) and context frequency (O'Connor 1985). MNE is counted as the most frequently occurring zone (Dobney and Reilly 1988) from left and right elements.

Taxonomic identifications

The following taxa were positively identified in the hand-recovered bone assemblage: cattle, *Bos* sp domestic; sheep, *Ovis* sp domestic; pig, *Sus* sp domestic; horse, *Equus caballus* sp domestic; dog, *Canis* sp domestic; cat, *Felis* sp domestic; and roe deer, *Capreolus capreolus* L. In addition a probable identification was made to red deer, cf *Cervus elaphus* L.

Species distribution and abundance

Period 2

Ranking the taxa from Period 2 in order of importance by the number of fragments gives the order: cattle, sheep, pig and equid (Table 29). Pig bones, however, were recovered from more contexts than those of sheep, indicating that they may have been more common (Table 32). An articulating partial skeleton makes up much of the dog bone assemblage. A fragment of antler identified to cf red deer has also been recorded from this period.

An equid lower molar ($M_{1/2}$) displays donkey-like characteristics of the enamel folds on the occlusal surface (Baxter 1998; Eisenmann 1986): the internal sulcus is V-shaped and the external sulcus does not penetrate between the metaflexid and entoflexid. Typically, horses have a U-shaped internal sulcus, and a deep external sulcus that partially penetrates between the metaflexid and entoflexid, and mules tend to have a more V-shaped internal sulcus than horses, but they also have a deep external sulcus (Armitage and Chapman 1979; Baxter 1998, 9). The size of tooth (Table 35), however, lies closer to the mean occlusal length, plotted by Eisenmann (1986, fig 20), of horses rather than donkeys. The morphology of the enamel folds on the specimen is characteristic of a donkey, but enamel patterns in equid teeth are variable (Armitage and Chapman 1979). In addition, a recent study of Iron Age horses from Hampshire revealed that the lower molars exhibited V-shaped internal sulci during the early stages of wear (Bendrey 2007). A single tooth is insufficient to provide a completely secure identification to species. All the other equid teeth from the site (Table 35) exhibit caballine characteristics (Baxter 1998; Eisenmann 1986).

The majority of the Period 2 assemblage derived from the fills of Enclosure 2 ditches (Table 31), most of which came from (40), the latest fill of F41 which produced a high concentration of later Roman domestic refuse, interpreted as the ditch being used as a midden. Cattle dominated the assemblage, possibly associated with disposal practise. Carnivore damage was recorded from this feature, indicating that the bone lay exposed for some time before burial, during which time dogs, or other carnivores, had opportunity to scavenge for food. The smaller bones of sheep are affected

61

to a greater extent by destruction from carnivore gnawing than the larger bones of cattle.

Sheep and pig are more common than cattle from the backfilling of Structure 1, in contrast to the ditch deposits from Enclosures 1 and 2. The fill of Enclosure 1 ditches produced a small quantity of bone as did the drainage system for Structure 1.

Period 3

Cattle is the most common taxon from Period 3 by number of fragments and context frequency, followed by sheep; but the higher representation of sheep mandibles and teeth by MNE (Table 33) compared to those of cattle indicate that sheep were the most common animal. Pig and horse are of only minor importance. A cat bone is also present.

The Period 3 assemblage derived from ditches and pits (Table 31). The largest sample derives from the eastern pit group within the confines of the Anglo-Saxon enclosures, within which cattle bones are the most common (Table 31).

Pit F219, at the south-west corner of Structure 3, produced twenty-eight fragments of bone (Table 31). Sheep is the only species identified from this feature, much of which is an articulating partial skeleton. The scapula, distal humerus and proximal radius of the skeleton are unfused, suggesting an age at death of less than 6–8 months (Silver 1969, 285). The profile, fill and stained edges of F219 were characteristic of a cess-pit (p 21). A sequence of Anglo-Saxon pits from Cherry Garden Hill (CTF 103) produced a number of articulating skeletons, mostly from cess-pits (Bendrey 2002). In one cess-pit was an articulating neonatal sheep skeleton.

	Period 2	Period 3	Period 4a	Period 4b	Period 4c	
Cattle	47 (45)	46	11	13	12	129
Sheep/goat†	26 (25)	33 (25)	10	13	3	85
(Sheep	4	9		1	1	15)
Pig	26 (24)	4	2	1		33
Equid†	11 (8)	4	2		4	21
(Horse	6	1				7)
Dog	9 (2)					9
Cat		1				1
Roe deer				1		1
cf Red deer	1					1
Cattle-sized	71	92	28	24	13	228
Sheep-sized	52	47	2	9	2	112
Indeterminate	16	18	19	4	69	126
Total	259	245	74	65	103	746

Table 29. Distribution of animal bone (NISP). †: sheep/goat and 'equid' include specimens identified at species level. (x): value in brackets is NISP adjusted for articulations (one group of articulating bones equals a count of 1).

Period	Feature	Total number of fragments	Carnivore gnawing	Burnt	Chop mark	Cut mark
2	Enclosure 2	211	8			
	Enclosure 1	13	1			6
	Infill Structure 1	26	2	1		1
	Drainage system, Structure 1	9	1			
3	Enclosure 3	42	1			
	Modification to Enclosure 3	8				
	Pits at southern corners of Enclosure 3	28				
	Eastern pit group	97	2	2	1	
	Western pit group	29				
	Central pit group	41	1			
4a	Structure 4	16				
	Structure 4, drainage gully	58	2	1		
4b	Medieval field ditch	41	2			1
	Medieval buried soil	24				
4c	Miscellaneous features	103				
Total		746	20	4	1	8

Table 30. Summary of some taphonomic data (NISP).

Period 4a

Sheep and cattle are the most common taxa from Period 4a: sheep elements are better represented by MNE, and cattle are recovered from more contexts (Tables 29, 30 and 33). Pig and horse are also present.

Bone was recovered from structural elements (post-holes and beam-slots) of Structure 4 and a gully surrounding part of it.

Period 4b

Cattle and sheep are the most important animals from Period 4b, equal in number and context frequency. Sheep are represented by a higher tooth count (Table 33), suggesting that they were more common. A pig and a roe deer fragment are also recorded.

Animal bone from Period 4b derived from field ditches (F3 and F308) and a buried soil (82).

Transverse cuts recorded on the posterior surface of a cattle proximal phalanx from this period are suggestive of skinning.

Age and sex data

A broad range of ages is represented by the Period 2 cattle (Table 34), indicating that during the Roman period cattle was a multi-purpose animal kept for secondary products, such as traction, and for meat. A female cattle pelvis, sexed following Grigson (1982, fig 1), is recorded from Period 3.

Period	2				3						4a		4b		4c
Feature	Enclosure 2	Enclosure 1	Infill Structure 1	Drainage system, Stucture 1	Enclosure 3	Modification to Enclosure 3	Pits at southern corners of Structure 3	Eastern pit group	Western pit group	Central pit group	Structure 4	Structure 4, drainage gully	Medieval field ditch	Medieval buried soil	Miscellaneous features
Cattle	39 (37)	5	3		3	2	11 (4)	30	3	8	5	6	11	2	12 (11)
Sheep	17 (16)		7	2	3			11 (10)		8	5	5	8	5	3
Pig	18 (17)	1	6 (5)	1	1			1		2	2		1		
Equid	8 (5)		3		1	1				2		2			4 (2)
Dog	8 (1)		1												
Cat					1										
Roe deer														1	
cf Red deer	1														
Cattle-sized	58	6	4	3	16	5	2	37	26	6	1	27	13	11	13
Sheep-sized	50		1	1	2		15	15		15	1	1	6	3	2
Indeterminate	12	1	1	2	15			3			2	17	1	3	69
Total	211	13	26	9	42	8	28	97	29	41	16	58	41	24	103

Table 31. Distribution of animal bone by sub-group (NISP). (x): value in brackets is NISP adjusted for articulations (one group of articulating bones equals a count of 1).

	Period 2		Period 3		Period 4a		Period 4b		Period 4c	
	cf	rf	cf	rf	cf	rf	cf	rf	cf	rf
Cattle	7	0.37	15	0.79	4	1.00	3	0.75	3	0.50
Sheep	6	0.32	9	0.47	3	0.75	3	0.75	3	0.50
Pig	7	0.37	3	0.16	2	0.50	1	0.25		
Equid	3	0.16	4	0.21	1	0.25			1	0.17
Dog	2	0.11								
Cat			1	0.05						
Roe deer							1	0.25		
cf Red deer	1	0.05								
Cattle-sized	10	0.53	15	0.79	3	0.75	3	0.75	4	0.67
Sheep-sized	5	0.26	8	0.42	2	0.50	2	0.50	2	0.33
Indeterminate	6	0.32	4	0.21	2	0.50	2	0.50	2	0.33
Total	19	1.00	19	1.00	4	1.00	4	1.00	6	1.00

Table 32. Distribution of animal bone by context frequency ('cf' is a count of the number of contexts which contained a taxon; 'rf' is the number as a proportion of the total number of bone-producing contexts (the relative frequency): O'Connor 1985).

The presence of animals aged around 8–10 years indicates that during Period 2 sheep were being kept for secondary products, such as wool and milk. Wool was an important product during the Roman period (Grant 1989, 139). Young animals are also present (Table 34), and may represent surplus males and infertile females culled for meat (*ibid*). Wool was also an important product during the Anglo-Saxon and medieval periods, as represented by the high proportion of mature animals (Table 34). A female sheep pelvis came from Period 3, sexed following Prummel and Frisch (1986, 575–6).

The presence of a number of neonatal pig remains from Period 2, including a mandible (Table 34) and a few post-cranial bones, suggests that pigs were being bred. Another pig mandible from Period 2 has been aged to 7–14 months. Pigs were killed before adulthood, as most of their value is in their carcass. Sexual data for pigs include one female pig lower canine from Period 2 and a female upper canine from Period 3 (Mayer and Brisbin 1988).

Ages from the horse teeth indicate all mature animals (Table 35).

Metrical data

A cattle metatarsal from the well (F300) has an estimated withers height of 1.226 metres, using the factor of Fock (von den Driesch and Boessneck 1974).

A reconstructed shoulder height of 45.2cm was calculated, following Clark (1995), from the metacarpal II of the dog skeleton from the Enclosure 2 ditches. This is fairly central within the size range of 23–72cm, recorded by Harcourt (1974) for Romano-British dogs, and is within the more restricted size ranges from other rural Roman sites in Kent (Bendrey 2008, 251–4; 2002).

	Cattle				Sheep				Pig			
	Period 2	Period 3	Period 4a	Period 4b	Period 2	Period 3	Period 4a	Period 4b	Period 2	Period 3	Period 4a	Period 4b
mandible	3	1	–	2	2	7	2	2	3	–	–	–1/–
DI	–/–	–/–	–/–	–/–	–/–	–/–	–/–	–/–	–/–	–/–	–/–	–/–
I	–/–	–/–	–/–	1/–	–/–	–/–	–/–	–/–	1/–	–/–	–/–	–/–
C	–/–	–/–	–/–	–/–	–/–	–/–	–/–	–/–	1/–	–/–	–/–	–/–
dP2	–/–	–/–	–/–	–/–	–/–	–/3	–/–	–/–	–/1	–/–	–/–	–/–
P2	–/–	–/–	–/–	–/–	–/–	–/1	–/–	–/–	–/–	–/–	–/–	–/–
dP3	–/–	–/–	–/–	–/–	–/2	–/3	–/–	–/–	–/1	–/–	–/–	–/–
P3	–/–	1/–	–/–	–/–	–/–	–/1	–/1	–/–	–/–	–/–	–/–	–/–
dP4	–/–	–/–	–/–	–/–	–/2	–/3	–/–	–/–	–/1	–/–	–/–	–/–
P4	–/1	–/–	–/–	–/–	–/–	–/2	–/2	–/1	–/–	–/–	–/–	–/–
M1	1/3	–/–	–/–	–/–	–/2	–/5	–/2	2/2	–/2	–/–	–/–	–/–
M1/2	–/–	–/–	–/–	–/–	–/–	–/–	–/–	–/–	–/–	–/–	–/–	–/–
M2	1/1	–/–	–/–	–/–	–/2	1/3	–/2	–/1	–/2	–/–	–/–	–/–
M3	–/2	1/–	–/–	–/–	1/3	1/2	–/3	–/–	–/–	–/–	1/–	–/–
cervical vertebra	3	1	–	–	–	–	–	–	–	–	–	–
thoracic vertebra	1	2	–	–	–	–	–	–	–	–	–	–
lumbar vertebra	–	–	–	–	–	–	–	–	–	–	–	–
sacrum	1	–	–	–	–	–	–	–	–	–	–	–
caudal vertebra	–	–	–	–	–	–	–	–	–	–	–	–
rib	–	–	–	–	1	–	–	–	–	–	–	–
scapula	1	1	–	–	2	1	–	–	3	1	–	–
humerus	4	1	1	–	–	2	–	2	2	–	–	–
radius	3	1	–	–	4	2	1	–	–	–	–	–
ulna	1	1	–	1	1	–	–	–	–	–	–	–
metacarpal	–	5	–	–	–	–	–	–	–	–	1	–
pelvis	2	2	1	1	–	1	–	1	–	–	–	–
femur	–	2	–	–	–	1	–	–	i	–	–	–
tibia	1	1	1	–	3	1	1	1	–	1	–	–
astragalus	1	–	–	–	–	–	–	–	–	–	–	–
calcaneum	–	–	–	2	–	1	–	–	–	–	–	–
metatarsal	–	1	1	2	1	2	–	1	–	–	–	–
1st phalanx	–	–	–	1	–	–	–	–	–	–	–	1
2nd phalanx	–	–	–	–	–	–	–	–	–	–	–	–
3rd phalanx	–	–	–	1	–	–	–	–	–	–	–	–

Table 33. Representation of skeletal elements of cattle, sheep and pig (MNE). Counting of teeth, eg 1/3, signifies loose teeth/teeth in mandibles.

Pathology and non-metrical variation

None of the three cattle lower third molars (M3) present exhibit the congenital absence or reduction of the hypoconulid.

A sheep mandible from Period 2, Structure 1, exhibits interdental attrition between M2 and M3. Another mandible, from the Period 3 eastern pit group, exhibits alveolar bone loss around P4 and M1 suggestive of periodontal disease. Another case of interdental attrition, between P4 and M1, is recorded from a Period 4b mandible.

A dog mandible from Enclosure 2 exhibits alveolar bone loss around the M1 alveolus: this tooth is missing, probably due to this bone loss.

Discussion

The small quantity of animal bones limits the information available, but some broad conclusions on species abundance can be made. Cattle is the most common and most important animal in the Roman deposits (Period 2), followed by pig and sheep in roughly equal numbers. In Period 3 cattle is also the most common taxon (by number of fragments and context frequency), but the higher representation of sheep by MNE suggests that sheep were the most common. MNE data suggests that sheep were also the most common from Periods 4a and 4b, followed by cattle. Pig and equid bones make only a minor contribution to the period assemblages, except for the role of pig in Period 2.

Analysis of element representation is limited due to the small sample size. Samples are too small to indicate any details of carcass-use, but the presence of most elements of the common animals suggests that the animals were slaughtered and processed on-site. The dearth of some elements, such as phalanges and vertebrae, can be explained due to preservational and recovery bias, as they are small bones or of low structural density.

The age data suggests that during the Roman period cattle and sheep were kept for meat and for secondary products, such as traction and wool. The sheep age data suggests that secondary products, probably wool, continued to be important during the Anglo-Saxon and medieval periods. The limited data for pigs indicates that they were being bred on site during the Roman period and that they were killed before maturity for meat. Horses were kept into maturity,

Period	Feature	Context	Taxon	P4	M1	M1/2	M2	M3	Suggested age	Notes
2	Enclosure 2	40	cattle	–	½	–	–	–	1–8 months	mandible
2	Enclosure 2	40	cattle	–	g	–	d	–	18–30 months†	loose teeth
2	Enclosure 2	40	cattle	–	l	–	k	k	senile	mandible
2	Enclosure 2	369	cattle	(k)	h	–	–	b	30–36 months	mandible
3	Eastern pit group	250	cattle	–	–	–	–	f	–	loose tooth
4c	Miscellaneous features	299	cattle	(j)	j	–	–	–	18–30 months†	mandible
4c	Miscellaneous features	299	cattle	–	–	g	–	–	–	loose tooth
2	Enclosure 2	40	sheep	(d)	–	–	–	–	2–6 months†	mandible
2	Enclosure 2	40	sheep	–	–	–	–	h	–	loose tooth
2	Infill, Structure 1	93	sheep	(l)	h	–	f	E	1–2 years	mandible
2	Infill, Structure 1	345	sheep	–	–	–	–	j	8–10 years	mandible
2	Infill, Structure 1	345	sheep	–	m	–	m	k	8–10 years	mandible
3	Eastern pit group	102	sheep	(h)	c	–	–	–	6–12 months†	mandible
3	Pits at southern corners of Structure 3	218	sheep	–	–	–	h	f	3–4 years	mandible
3	Eastern pit group	339	sheep	–	j	–	h	–	–	mandible
3	Eastern pit group	339	sheep	j	l	–	h	g	6–8 years	mandible
3	Central pit group	343	sheep	½	g	–	–	–	–	mandible
3	Central pit group	350	sheep	–	–	–	f	–	–	loose tooth
3	Enclosure 3	424	sheep	(g)	e	–	–	–	–	mandible
4a	Structure 4 drainage gully	114	sheep	j	k	–	h	f	3–4 years	mandible
4a	Structure 4	318	sheep	–	–	–	–	e	3–4 years	mandible
4a	Structure 4	318	sheep	h	k	–	h	g	6–8 years	mandible
4b	Medieval field ditch	242	sheep	–	g	–	–	–	–	loose tooth
4b	Medieval buried soil	268	sheep	–	k	–	–	–	–	mandible
4b	Medieval buried soil	268	sheep	–	–	–	d	–	–	loose tooth
4b	Medieval buried soil	268	sheep	–	g	–	j	–	–	mandible
2	Enclosure 2	40	pig	–	d	–	½	–	7–14 months	mandible
2	Infill, Structure 1	439	pig	(E)	–	–	–	–	0–2 months	mandible
4a	Structure 4	347	pig	–	–	–	–	c	–	loose tooth

Table 34. Cattle, sheep and pig toothwear data. Suggested ages have been awarded to mandibles with at least one tooth *in situ* following Halstead (1985), Payne (1973) and Hambleton (1999). †: ages assigned through extrapolation of toothwear with reference to Grant 1982 (tables 2–3).

Phase	Feature	Context	Tooth	Length (mm) VdD	Breadth (mm) vdD	Crown height (mm) Lev	Age (years)
2	Enclosure 2	40	M¹ᐟ²	25.8	25.7	55.3	7–9½
2	Enclosure 2	301	P²†		24.5	57.1	6–7
2	Enclosure 2	301	P³†	29.5	24	72.9	5–6
2	Enclosure 2	301	P⁴†			77.8	5–6
2	Enclosure 2	301	M¹‡			71.1	5–6
2	Enclosure 2	301	M²‡		23.8	77.9	5–6
2	Infill Structure 1	345	M₁ᐟ₂	26.3	14.1	70.7	5–6
3	Modification to Enclosure 3	33	M₂	26.9	16.7	64.8	5–6

Table 35. Equid teeth, crown height data (after Levine 1982). vdD: measurements follow von den Driesch (1976, figs 6b and 19b). Lev: measurements follow Levine (1982, fig 2). †: articulating right toothrow. ‡: articulating left toothrow.

as work animals. There is no evidence to suggest that they had been consumed.

Other animals represented include horse, dog, cat, and two species of deer. The antler fragment from Period 2 is not evidence for hunting as shed antler could have been collected as a raw material. The medieval roe deer mandible is, however, evidence for hunting. Grant (1988, 186; 1989, 144) suggests that medieval populations had a greater reliance on wild resources, compared to earlier periods, due to the inadequacies of the farming system to feed an expanding population.

Environmental samples

Enid Allison

Eleven bulk soil samples were taken from the site, totalling 217 litres in volume. Volumes of individual samples ranged between 2 and 55 litres, but were usually between 10 and 20 litres. Details are held in archive.

Methods

The bulk samples were processed by bucket flotation to produce a washover onto 0.5mm mesh. The residue was washed through nested 1mm and 2mm sieves. Washovers and residues were air-dried. Residues were sorted for biological material and artefacts and washovers examined briefly under a low-powered microscope (x10).

One sample (sample 8a, context 349, the primary fill of pit F344) was treated slightly differently due to its small size and also to determine whether organic material preserved by waterlogging was present. This sample was washed to 0.3mm and separated into fractions by carrying out bucket flotation to produce a washover and a residue (both collected on 0.3mm mesh). The washover and residue were initially examined wet under a low-powered binocular microscope (x10 to x20), then air-dried.

Results

Two samples were examined from deposits from the flue of Structure 1 (samples 9 and 10 from contexts 399 and 500,

Period 2). Both produced substantial well-preserved charred cereal and weed seed assemblages which are reported upon in detail below.

Sample 2 (context 186) was taken from the fill of F187 which was originally thought to be a possible hearth. The sample residue contained many fragments of calcined bone, daub or burnt earth, pottery sherds and hobnails indicating that this was a cremation deposit. A tooth fragment possibly of a pig was present among the calcined remains but it is not unusual to find animal bone cremated along with human remains. The washover from the sample was relatively large. It consisted mainly of charcoal, but included a small, well-preserved assemblage of charred cereal grains and weed seeds.

The residue from Sample 4 (context 254, fill of gully F255, associated with Structure 3, Period 3) consisted almost entirely of shell. The majority of the shell fragments were of mussel (*Mytilus edulis* L), fragments of cockle shell (*Cerastoderma edule* L) were common, and there were small amounts of oyster (*Ostrea edulis* L), winkle (*Littorina littorea* (L)) and baltic tellin (*Macoma balthica* (L)). The last species is likely to have been harvested accidentally with the other edible shellfish. Land snails were more common in the washover than in other sampled deposits from the site, possibly because the amounts of shell present had raised the pH of the sediment, allowing better preservation of calcareous material. The sample also contained a small amount of charred cereal grain, a fruit stone, and small fragments of mammal bone, some of which had been burnt.

Samples from three pits that were probably associated with Structure 3 (Period 3) all produced remnants of domestic waste including pottery and daub. Charred cereal grains, pulses and other seeds were abundant in Sample 1 from the lower fill of F141 (context 140). A few small fragments of large mammal bone, some of which had been burnt, and traces of mussel shell were also present.

The residue from Sample 7, (context 339, fill of pit F340, Period 3) consisted largely of yellow powdery concretions of uncertain origin (around 75 per cent); these did not look like typical faecal concretions and may be the result of some undetermined post-depositional process. It is possible, however, that they do represent very poorly preserved faecal material. Other remains were sparse and fragmentary, consisting of small amounts of charred cereal grain and seeds, large mammal and fish bone, including common eel (*Anguilla anguilla* (L)), several fragments of bird vertebrae, and traces of oyster shell. A small number of similar yellow powdery concretions were found in Sample 3 from context 218 (the fill of pit F219, Period 3), along with a few charred cereal remains and unidentifiable fragments of large mammal and fish bone.

Two samples from a putative cess-pit (F344, Period 3) were examined; Sample 8a from the primary fill (349) and Sample 8 from the upper fill (343). Sample 8a produced a washover that consisted chiefly of small fragments of charcoal and the mineralised remains of faeces, the latter supporting the interpretation of the feature as a cess-pit. A few fragmentary mineralised seeds, fly puparia, millipedes and undiagnostic fragments of beetle cuticle were present, together with poorly preserved fragments of charred cereal grain. The residue contained many small and fragmentary fish bones such as are often found in cess deposits. Few of these were identifiable. Very small fragments of large mammal bone, mouse or vole and amphibian bones, a tracheal ring of a bird and earthworm egg capsules were present. No biological remains preserved by waterlogging were seen. A single sherd of pottery was recovered along with small quantities of hammerscale. Sample 8 from a later fill also contained small amounts of the mineralised remains of faeces, along with fragments of large mammal, mouse or vole and fish bone, a few charred cereal grains, slag and flake hammerscale.

A sample from the well (Sample 6, context 299) produced a substantial assemblage of charred plant remains, including cereal grains, pulses and other seeds, together with a lesser quantity of uncharred seeds. Bone of large mammals was relatively common, and there were a few fragments of small mammal and fish bone. Several sherds of pottery, a small amount of daub, and brick or tile fragments were recovered.

Details of the contents of all the residues and washovers are held in archive. In general, the survival of mineralised seeds, invertebrates, molluscs and animal bone was poor, and offered little information; however, five samples produced significant assemblages of charred plant remains, which are discussed below.

Charred plant remains

Ruth Pelling

Methods

All washovers were scanned under a binocular microscope at magnification of x10 to x20. Charred material including both grain and charcoal was noted in all samples. Five samples were thought to contain sufficient material to merit further analysis: two from Structure 1 and three from a Roman cremation (F187), a possibly Anglo-Saxon well (F300) and a pit (F141). The selected samples were sorted fully under a binocular microscope. Any quantifiable seeds and chaff

extracted were identified based on morphological criteria and by comparison with modern reference material held at the Oxford University Museum of Natural History.

Results

The detail results of the analysis are displayed in Tables 36 and 37. Nomenclature and taxonomic order follows Clapham *et al* (1989).

Structure 1

Two samples were examined from the flue of Structure 1 (contexts 399 and 500; Period 2). Both assemblages were mixed, with grain, chaff and weed seeds. *Triticum spelta* (spelt wheat) and *Hordeum vulgare* (barley) are the principal crops represented, although some *Avena* sp (oats) grains and *Secale cereale* (rye) rachis may also be from cultivated crops. The *Triticum* seems to outnumber the *Hordeum vulgare* and is likely to have been the cereal being processed in the structure. The *Hordeum vulgare* may be present as a contaminant or as the waste from a previous processing episode. The ratio of *Triticum* glume bases to *Triticum* grain is approximately equal in context 399, while the glume bases outnumber grain in context 500 by approximately 3:1. Even if the bulk of the indeterminate grain is of *Triticum spelta*, glume bases are still well represented. As grain always survives charring better than chaff (Boardman and Jones 1990) the glume bases may be under-represented in relation to grain, but not *vice-versa*. This would imply that while context 399 could contain whole spikelets, context 500 must include additional chaff. In context 399 weed seeds were more numerous than grain or chaff but included a large number of cereal-sized *Bromus* subsect *Eubromus* (brome grass) grain. The weed seeds are dominated by large seeded species such as *Bromus* and *Agrostemma githago* (corn cockle), or species that produce composite seed heads such as *Anthemis cotula* (stinking mayweed) or *Tripleurospermum inodorum* (scentless mayweed). These weed seeds are likely to have been harvested with the spelt crop and have remained with the grain after the earlier stages of sieving and winnowing. Many of the *Bromus* grains had actually germinated and may have been a tolerated impurity of the grain. The range of species represented is limited, all of which are arable weeds commonly recovered from Romano-British sites. *Rumex acetosella* suggests the cultivation of light acidic sandy soils as are present in the Medway area, although *Anthemis cotula* suggests the cultivation of some heavier chalk soils.

Samples from other features

Three further samples produced significant assemblages of charred plant remains. Sample 2 came from Roman cremation F187, Sample 1 from Anglo-Saxon pit F141, and Sample 6 from the well F300 (*see* p 27). This third sample produced a large assemblage of grain, chaff, pulses and weeds. Due to time constraints absolute counts were not given for weed seeds. All species noted were identified but they are recorded by relative abundance with an approximate minimum total given. This provides sufficient information to demonstrate that weeds formed the greatest proportion of the assemblage, although grain was also numerous, and to provide a species list for weeds. Contexts 140 and 186 are grain-rich with little or no chaff and moderate quantities of weeds. Context 186 produced a small assemblage, however so the proportions of the different components cannot be

assumed to be truly representative. Pulses were present as minor components in contexts 140 and 299.

The range of cereal species is consistent in all three samples with *Hordeum vulgare* the most numerous species identified by grain, and *Secale cereale* and *Avena* sp also common typical species of Anglo-Saxon period deposits. The *Hordeum vulgare* appears to be a hulled six-row variety. *Avena* sp outnumbered *Secale cereale* in context 299. *Triticum* sp was infrequent in all three samples. The occasional hulled *Triticum*

	Sample	399	500
	Feature	Structure 1	Structure 1
	Feature type	Flue	Flue
	Date	Roman	Roman
	Volume (l)	10	10
Cereal grain	spelt wheat, germinated grain	15	7
Triticum spelta	spelt wheat	31	16
Triticum spelta	spelt/emmer wheat	2	4
Triticum spelta/dicoccum	wheat, germinated grain	6	4
Triticum sp	wheat	17	11
Triticum sp	barley, hulled asymmetric grain	3	
Hordeum vulgare	barley, hulled	8	9
Hordeum vulgare	barley, hulled germinated grain		1
Hordeum vulgare	oats	4	6
Avena sp	indeterminate grain	28	45
Cerealia indet	detached embryo	3	2
Cerealia indet	sprouted embryo		2
Cereal chaff			
Triticum spelta	spelt wheat glume base	43	24
Triticum spelta/dicoccum	spelt/emmer wheat glume base	52	107
Triticum sp	hexaploid wheat rachis		2
Secale cereale	rye rachis		1
Cereal size	culm node		1
Pulses			
Vicia/Pisum sp	vetch/vetchling/pea	1	1
Weeds			
Silene sp	campion, capsule tip		2
Agrostemma githago	corn cockle	14	4
cf *Agrostemma githago*	cf corn cockle		2
Rumex acetosella	sheep's sorrel		2
Rumex sp	docks	1	
Polygonum aviculare	knotgrass	1	
Plantago lanceolata/media	plantain		1
Galium aparine	goosegrass		1
Veronica sp			1
Medicago/Trifolium/Lotus sp	medick/clover/trefoil	15	5
Anthemis cotula	stinking mayweed	7	3
Tripleurospermum inodorum	stinking mayweed	2	2
Lapsana communis	nipplewort	2	1
Compositae			2
Bromus subsect *Eubromus*	brome grass	120	46
Bromus subsect *Eubromus*	brome grass, germinated	7	22
Gramineae	grass, large seeded	9	9
Gramineae	grass, small seeded	3	

Table 36. Charred plant remains from the Roman corn-drier.

grain and glume base in the Anglo-Saxon deposits is likely to derive from residual Roman contamination. The presence of rye and free-threshing wheat in the Roman cremation suggests the presence of intrusive Anglo-Saxon material in the deposit. The Anglo-Saxon *Triticum* is likely to be free-threshing. Given the inherent difficulties in distinguishing between *Triticum* and *Secale cereale* grain the number of *Secale cereale* grains may be higher than recorded. Equally, a large number of rachis fragments could not be positively identified as either *Secale cereale* or *Hordeum vulgare*. Several of the *Hordeum vulgare* grains in context 299 showed signs of germination.

While chaff is less numerous than grain in context 299 the number of rachis fragments is significant when it is considered that the cereals involved, *Hordeum vulgare* and *Secale cereale*, are free-threshing. In free-threshing cereals the grain easily falls free from the chaff during threshing which is followed by winnowing and sieving (Hillman's stages 5 to 7, 1981; 1994). These early stages of processing are often conducted in threshing barns near the arable fields, away from the site. Chaff, particularly from free-threshing cereals, is often also under-represented in archaeological assemblages as it survives charring less well than the grain (Boardman and Jones 1990). The number of rachis, including basal rachis in samples from context 299 would therefore suggest that whole ears or straw may be included, possibly of both *Secale cereale* and *Hordeum vulgare*.

In addition to the cereals occasional pulses represent another cultivated crop. The majority of pulses lack the hila and testa necessary for identification to species. One individual does display the remains of a lozenge shaped hila characteristic of *Vicia sativa* (vetch), although preservation is poor. In size the seed was appropriate for smaller cultivated varieties although does fall in the overlap zone between wild and cultivated. It was recorded as *Vicia* cf *sativa subsp sativa* (cultivated vetch).

The majority of the weed species could derive from arable fields, some of which have particular associations (Silverside 1977; Godwin 1975). *Fallopia convolvulus* (black bindweed) is particularly associated with spring sown barley. *Lithospermum arvense* (corn gromwell), *Galium aparine* (goosegrass) and *Anthemis cotula* (stinking mayweed) are more generally associated with autumn sown crops, and *L arvense* with autumn sown rye. The wild vetches (*Vicia/Lathyrus* sp) tend to commonly occur as weedy forms of cultivated vetches. *Galium aparine* and *Anthemis cotula* tend to be characteristic of heavy calcareous soils, although there is also good evidence for light sandy and acid soils from *Papaver somniferum* (opium poppy), *Stellaria gramineae* (lesser stichwort), *Montia fontana* (blinks), and *Rumex acetosella* (sheep's sorrel). Both soil types are likely to have been cultivated. A large number of *Sambucus nigra* (elder) seeds from the well sample were not charred. The seeds of this species are particularly robust and do tend to survive in an uncharred state on Anglo-Saxon and medieval sites (eg Murphy 1985) or will survive in partly waterlogged conditions where less robust seeds do not. They are unlikely to be present as weeds of an arable crop but may have been

thrown or dropped into the well as a bunch of fruit, either deliberately or by accident from an overhanging shrub. Similarly the occasional fragments of *Corylus avellana* nutshell cannot be derived from arable weeds but may represent food waste or fuel.

Discussion

One of the questions posed by the archaeologists was whether or not Structure 1 was in fact a corn-drier. A survey of charred plant remains from twenty-one British corn-driers was made by Van der Veen (1989) in which she assessed their possible function. She concluded that they were multi-functional structures concerned with the roasting of germinated grain for malt production and the preparation of grain prior to storage/consumption. While both barley and spelt wheat were present in corn-driers, malting always seemed to have involved spelt wheat, for example at Catsgore, Somerset (Hillman 1982) and Bancroft Roman villa, Milton Keynes (Pearson and Robinson 1994). Pliny documents the use of wheat for beer by the Romans (*Nat Hist Book* xviii).

The malting process involves the forced germination of grain previously steeped in water in order to modify the endosperm to a certain stage (roughly when the sprout is the length of the grain). The germination process is then stopped by roasting or 'curing' the sprouted grain in hot air. If the grain used is spelt wheat it could be expected that the glume bases and sprouts could be removed together after 'curing'. The waste product would then include glume bases, sprouted embryos (coleoptiles) and occasional grain, some of which may have germinated. Cereal-sized weed seeds and seed heads might also be present. Accidental burning during curing would result in glumes and grains in similar numbers with the majority of grain (Van der Veen suggests an arbitrary figure of 75 per cent) showing signs of germination.

The use of corn-driers in the processing of grain for consumption/storage covers a range of possible stages. Reynolds and Langley (1979) suggested the structures were not generally suitable for drying clean grain, while the large-scale storage of de-hulled grain is unlikely outside of military granaries as the grain survives better in spikelet form. It is possible however that the structures could be used to recover spoilt harvests, for de-husking prior to milling/consumption, or for the processing of greencorn. In these cases accidental burning would result in approximately equal numbers of grain and glume bases with occasional coleoptiles and sprouted grain. Processing waste would consist of glume bases, and occasional coleoptiles and grain, some of which may have sprouted. The significance of the use of corn-driers in any of these processes is that it implies cereal processing on a large scale.

Structure 1 certainly produced sufficient cereal processing waste to assume a major cereal processing activity was taking place. In practice, archaeobotanical assemblages usually represent material burnt as refuse or as fuel, rather than the 'in-use' assemblages. In the case of a corn-drier this could be the waste from a processing episode. It is therefore

		Context	186	299	140
		Feature	187		141
		Feature type	Cremation	Well	Pit
		Date	Roman	?Anglo-Saxon	Anglo-Saxon
		Volume	10	50	20
Cereal grain					
Triticum sp	wheat, free-threshing		3	8	1
Triticum spelta/dicoccum	spelt/emmer wheat				1
Triticum sp	wheat, indeterminate		1	9	4
Hordeum vulgare	barley, hulled asymmetric		4	19	39
Hordeum vulgare	barley, hulled asymmetric, germinated			1	
Hordeum vulgare	barley, hulled straight		2	10	20
Hordeum vulgare	barley, hulled straight, germinated			5	
Hordeum vulgare	barley, hulled		16	71	101
Hordeum vulgare	barley, hulled germinated			19	
Hordeum vulgare	barley			163	54
Hordeum vulgare	barley, germinated			9	
Secale cereale	rye		18	33	96
Secale cereale/Triticum sp	rye/wheat			39	1
Secale cereale/Triticum sp	rye/wheat, germinated			1	
Avena sp	oats			182	15
Cerealia indet	indeterminate grain		8	260	35
Cereal chaff					
Triticum spelta	spelt wheat glume base			1	
Hordeum vulgare	barley rachis			33	1
Secale cereale	rye rachis			33	3
Secale cereale/Hordeum vulgare	rye/barley rachis			70	
Cerealia indet	indeterminate rachis			20	5
Cerealia indet	indeterminate basal rachis			9	
Cerealia indet	detached embroyo			6	4
Cereal size	culm node			8	
Pulses					
Vicia cf *sativa* subsp *sativa*	cf fodder vetch			1	
Vicia/Pisum sp	vetch/bean/pea			16	4
Weeds					
Papaver somniferum	opium poppy			x	
Papaver sp	poppy			x	
Silene dioica	red campion			x	
Agrostemma githago	corn cockle		5	xxx	8
cf *Agrostemma githago*	corn cockle				3
Stellaria media agg	chickweed		5	x	2
Stellaria gramineae	lesser stichwort			x	
Montia fontana subsp *chondrosperma*	blinks		3		
Chenopodium album	fat hen		3	xxx	1
Atriplex sp	orache			x	
Chenopodiaceae				x	1
Malva sylvestris	mallow				1
Vicia/Lathyrus sp	vetch/vetching/tare		1	xxx	33
Medicago/Trifolium/Lotus sp	medick/Clover/Trefoil			x	2
Torilis japonica	upright hedge parsley		1		
Umbelliferae				x	1
Polygonum aviculare	knotgrass		1	x	1
Fallopia convolvulus	black bindweed			xx	
Rumex acetosella agg	sheep's sorrel				
Rumex sp	docks			xx	1
Corylus avellana	hazel nut shell fragments			x	
cf *Anagallis* type	pimpernel type			x	
Lithospermum arvense	corn gromwell			x	
Galeopsis sp	hemp-nettle			x	

		186	299	140
	Context	186	299	140
	Feature	187		141
	Feature type	Cremation	Well	Pit
	Date	Roman	?Anglo-Saxon	Anglo-Saxon
	Volume	10	50	20
Plantago media/lanceolata	plantain		x	
Galium aparine	goosegrass	1	xx	8
Sambucus nigra	elderberry, uncharred		xxx	
Compositae			x	1
Anthemis cotula	stinking mayweed		xxx	4
Tripleurospermum inodorum	scentless mayweed		x	
Lapsana communis	nipplewort		xxx	
Carex sp	sedges		x	1
Bromus subsect *Eubromus*	brome grass	5	xx	5
Gramineae	grass, large seeded	2	xxx	5
Gramineae	grass, large seeded		xx	3
Indet	indeterminate seed	2		5
	Total weeds	26	1000 plus	86

Table 37. Charred plant remains from other features. x: present. xx: common. xxx: abundant.

possible to conjecture that the assemblage from Structure 1 represents fuel, derived from the by-product of a major event, and it is likely that the structure is a corn-drier. Establishing the processing activities for which the corn-drier was used is more complex however, and it is likely that it was used for more than one purpose. The presence of grain other than spelt wheat would suggest that we do not simply have the residue of malting, although this does not mean some malting residue is not included. The number of germinated large grass seeds is interesting and might suggest that they were germinated with grain destined for malt. It is reasonable to expect sprouted weeds and only a few sprouted grain in the waste product of curing as the good, sprouted grain would be used for the malt. The low number of coleoptiles would argue against malting as the main source of material however, although this could be explained by preservation biases. Certainly it seems likely that the material present is essentially fuel rather than product (given the large ratio of glumes and weeds to grain) some or all of which is derived from crop processing activities within the oven. The use of cereal processing waste, particularly chaff, as fuel for all forms of roasting or parching grain, especially malting is suggested by Hillman (1982) and is documented for the later medieval period by Markham (1681). The straw and glume bases would be easily available and would not affect the taste of the resulting malt or dried grain, particularly important for beer production.

The Roman cremation sample (context 186) may represent *in situ* burning, in which case the occasional seeds and chaff are likely to be present as small amounts of waste thrown on the fire, or possibly deliberately used as kindling rather than food being cooked. However, the crop species present include species (free-threshing wheat, rye and oats) more characteristic of the Anglo-Saxon and later periods suggesting this context contains later intrusive material.

The pit and well assemblages must represent secondary deposits. The mix of cereals suggests mixed deposits of more than one harvest; oats and barley can be cultivated together successfully as a spring sown 'drage', but rye cannot have been grown with them being an exclusively autumn sown crop. It is likely therefore that both deposits represent more than one harvest and processing episode, either mixed during burning or at the point of deposition. Context 299 in particular may contain whole ears or straw of rye and/or barley. Weed assemblages of the rye and the barley, oats or drage seem to be represented and suggest the cultivation of both heavy and light sandy soils.

While the deposits are mixed, barley seems to be the dominant cereal in both Anglo-Saxon samples. Barley and oats may have been grown together as a drage. This practice is known from later historical sources (eg Markham 1681) and there is archaeobotanical evidence that they were grown as drage in the Anglo-Saxon period (Campbell 1994). Given the limited number of samples it is impossible to speculate as to the real importance of barley or to its uses. The presence of rachis might suggest that it was intended for fodder, which would require less processing than cereal for human consumption. It is possible that the dominance of barley is due to the site being concerned with stock rearing rather than arable production for human consumption which would normally favour wheats. Rye was not cultivated in all areas during the Anglo-Saxon period and for example is very rarely recorded in Hampshire (Green 1991). As yet it is not known if rye cultivation reflects soil types (it tends to perform well on soils where wheat crops will perform badly) or cultural choice. Too little is known about the Anglo-Saxon cereal economy of Kent to establish how important a crop it was in the area, although it is recorded from late Saxon deposits at Northfleet, Kent (Pelling 2001). When rye is recorded archaeologically it tends to produce large assemblages of rachis, particularly so for a free-threshing cereal. As it produces a long straw this is often taken to reflect its use for thatching or for malting mats (for example at West Cotton, Campbell 1994). Such uses could be possible for the Wainscott rye. Historic evidence certainly demonstrates such uses (eg Markham 1681) and recently studied examples of medieval smoked blackened rye thatch are known (Letts 2000).

Conclusions

Although the number of charred plant assemblages from Wainscott was limited they did produce good quantities of seeds and chaff and do provide some evidence for the arable agriculture at the site in both the Roman and Anglo-Saxon periods. The crops grown are generally appropriate for the periods, with spelt wheat dominating the Roman samples and hulled barley, oats and rye numerous in the Anglo-Saxon period. The Roman cremation sample conversely contains cereals more typical of the Anglo-Saxon period, suggesting the presence of some later contamination. The paucity of wheat and dominance of barley and rye in the Anglo-Saxon samples may be associated with stock rearing, or may reflect a local preference for rye rather than wheat.

It is not possible to convincingly establish the function of Structure 1 although it is probable that it is a 'corn-drier' in that it was probably used for large-scale cereal processing of some type. The assemblages are likely to represent the fuel used in the corn-drier, which itself is likely to be derived from past processing episodes. Malting and processing of cereals prior to storage/consumption might be represented. The use of chaff as fuel might reflect its availability, lack of need for its use as fodder (ie available alternative fodder sources), lack of alternative fuel types, or the nature of the processing event it was used for.

The three other samples provide evidence for a greater range of cereal species and other crops, and provide some evidence for the cultivation of both heavy and light acid soils. As mixed secondary deposits they provide no clues as to the processing phases or uses of the cereals, other than that whole ears or lengths of straw of rye and/or barley are included.

5

Discussion

Jonathan Rady and Christopher Sparey-Green

Prehistoric *(Period 1)*

At the Four Elms roundabout site little *in situ* prehistoric activity was encountered although elsewhere on the road project some isolated features and finds were identified. A late Bronze Age metalwork hoard was also recovered by metal detectorists, though this material has not been studied in any detail (*see* p 5, footnote 2). The main site produced unstratified pottery and worked stone debris; one pit did contain middle Bronze Age pottery (F270), suggesting casual occupation, while the lithic assemblage is suggestive of late Neolithic/early Bronze Age presence close by.

Roman *(Period 2)*

The earliest Roman activity seems to consist simply of two isolated pits of second- or early third-century date, possibly features on the periphery of a site to the north. The main activity falls within a fairly restricted period of the third century AD and comprises two enclosures associated with the heated building, Structure 1.

Enclosures 1 and 2 differed considerably in their character. Enclosure 1 was very restricted in size, enclosing an area of only 70m^2.

Enclosure 2 encompassed a much greater area and, if of rectilinear or quadrilateral plan and symmetrical about a single south-western entrance, could have enclosed at least 0.50 hectare. The disparity in area to Enclosure 1 suggests that Enclosure 2 represents a new scheme, incorporating the first enclosure, Structure 1 and a large open area in their vicinity. The quantities of pottery in the southern enclosure ditch and the identification of trampled soils in the same area (Context 42/43, adjacent to Enclosure 2) suggests some domestic activity but also use as a cattle enclosure, the foot-prints on one side of the ditch suggesting animals were perhaps drinking from it. Cattle or horse hoof impressions of Roman date have previously been identified at Canterbury (Bennett 1978, 275) and, further afield, at the rural settlement at Flögeln, Germany where trampling occurred in a similar context to Wainscott (Haio Zimmermann 1978, 154).

An enclosure of the dimensions of Enclosure 2 would be comparable to other rural sites known from air photographs in east Kent where small square, subsquare or rectangular enclosures have been identified on the chalk downs, these having sides of between 70 and 130m long. Others have been identified as cropmarks in the area south-west of the Four Elms roundabout, close to Higham. Such ditched areas could have contained small family-sized subsistence farmsteads but in the present case the substantial heated structure suggests either a more specialised purpose or that this was the working area of a more substantial farmstead or villa nearby. This hypothesis would require the existence of an adjacent higher status dwelling and/or farm buildings on the unexcavated north or eastern sides, the drier thus lying in front of, and to one side of, a more substantial building facing south or west. In the case of a villa, a western entrance would be unlikely, the preferred layout being with an entrance on the south-east and an approach to the main building's frontage on the sunnier and warmer aspect. The western entrance here would suggest a more utilitarian enclosure opening onto the land to the west, the relatively short-lived occupation and general lack of features within the enclosure, but with a concentration of domestic debris in one area, being atypical of an intensively occupied or long-lived settlement. This interpretation would also fit the generally low status of the recovered ceramics and other finds (p 41). An enclosure connected with industrial and farming activity during the late second to third century is most likely.

The one major building, Structure 1, conforms to a standard type of heated building usually interpreted as corn-driers or malting ovens but possibly serving a variety of purposes. The building may have been furnished with an original short furnace which was then lengthened in a second phase and an internal baffle inserted at the end of the sub-floor flue. There also appears to have been a threshold in the south wall, opposite the furnace (Fig 5). This was later infilled, suggesting a major rebuilding either blocking the doorway or the raising of the door step. This change may have coincided with the renewal of the furnace or the final phase in which the flues were infilled with rubble and a solid floor created.

Drainage of the site seems to have been a problem and a gully led south-west from the stoke-hole into a larger drain that in turn emptied into the enclosure ditch. The placing of a drying building in a location subject to flooding seems hardly practical but invites comparison with the situation at the Halstock villa, Dorset where ovens or driers also had their flue channels connected to drains (Lucas 1993, 46). This was presumed to derive from the need, on a clay site with a high water table similar to Wainscott, to drain off any water that intermittently flooded the furnace when not in use, perhaps in the winter period.

As at Halstock, ovens or driers do not need to be free-standing structures but could have been internal features of larger barns, perhaps with the intention of providing some background warmth to the building, albeit while adding to the risk of fire. The slight linear features to the north-east of Structure 1 might have formed part of a very simple building but are more likely to have been no more than a fence or open-sided shed that, with the truncated Enclosure 1 on the south, separated the drier and four-post Structure 2 from the remainder of the interior of the enclosure. Driers similar in size and plan to the present example, however, would be more likely to have been constructed as free-standing, roofed structures.

The only general study of the range of drying buildings in Roman Britain is not comprehensive and does not cover issues such as the relationship to ovens and furnaces or to the smallest and simplest hypocaust buildings (Morris 1979, 5–15). The idea of Pitt-Rivers when first encountering below-ground furnaces with heating platforms on Cranborne Chase was that these were simple rural versions of domestic hypocausts, an idea now discounted but yet worthy of reconsideration (as for example at Woodcutts; Pitt-Rivers 1887, 29–31). Heated structures of this general character have usually been described as 'corn-driers' but they could have served a variety of purposes including use as malting ovens or even for the preliminary drying of clay products; they should perhaps be given some more general nomenclature such as 'small heated buildings'. They range from simple furnaces with linear flues, which are no more than large domestic ovens, to the larger and more elaborate examples often of a T-shaped plan or more elaborate multiple channel form. At the upper limits lie the substantial circular buildings with solid floors and pillared chambers like small hypocausts, both exemplified at Great Casterton (Corder 1954, 19–24; 1961, fig 24). Where environmental evidence is lacking it may not be possible to resolve the question about the use of such structures. The present square within square plan is a less common form and raises questions as to the system of air circulation and the presence of perhaps a central chimney. It might be compared to the substantial building at Foxhole Farm, Hertford, a well preserved drier used as a pattern by Peter Reynolds for his experiment at Butser Hill (Reynolds and Langley 1979). This structure of chalk and flint was of U-shaped plan with a central chamber, the floor of which was slightly higher than the surrounding flue and was accessed by vents through the wall. The latter detail was

not observed at Wainscott, possibly because of damage or truncation to the structure. Another structure similar in its plan and size was identified within an enclosure of a Roman settlement at Longthorpe (Dannell and Wild 1987, 78). This drier was of a square within square form, the channel nearest to and at right angles to the flue being later blocked to create a U-shaped plan with a solid central platform. As at Wainscott the firing chamber was to the north and showed evidence of rebuilding and extension. No environmental study of the burnt debris was carried out but the use of half a quernstone in the extended firing chamber suggests the processing of grain and preparation of flour in the vicinity. A date in the third century AD for the use of the drier places this roughly contemporary to Wainscott.

Many rural sites in southern Britain have produced examples of small heated structures, a prime instance being those within buildings 3.5, 3.6 and 3.13 of the late Roman road-side settlement at Catsgore (Leech 1982, 65–9). These produced examples of respectively, T-shaped, H-shaped and Y-shaped channel systems, the potential area of the heated floors being between approximately 6 to 9 square metres, similar to that for the drier buildings at Wainscott and Foxhole Farm. The Catsgore examples produced sprouted wheat and have therefore been interpreted as malting ovens for beer-making but it should be noted that the H-shaped drier was accompanied by a quern in place on the paving beside it. From a very different location, the settlement at Rockbourne Down on the chalk downs of Cranborne Chase has produced examples of single and double-T form channels and H-plan flue systems in small house plots or enclosures of the late Roman period (Sumner 1913, 38; Bowen 1990, 67–8). No plan of any surrounding structures was forthcoming but the first of these had a heated floor area of approximately 18 square metres and was presumed by Sumner to have served as a hypocaust heating a dwelling, accompanied by a more standard-sized T-shaped drier interpreted as a bakehouse. The H-shaped drier, malting kiln or oven superseded a small ditched enclosure and lay within a later 35 hectare enclosure around a spring at the head of a coombe. The combination of drier and enclosure might invite comparison with Wainscott but the scale and form of the enclosure are markedly different. The size of the largest drier at Rockbourne suggests that this was capable of processing large quantities of grain or, less probably, of serving as a small bath-house.

A number of small heated structures have been identified in Kent but few definite drying buildings or ovens. The villa at Thurnham has produced a stone-built drier of an elaborate T-shaped plan, this structure being of similar scale to the Wainscott building (Union Rail Limited 1999, 8). Significantly, this structure lay within a partially ditched area on the far eastern perimeter of the site and lay on the site of, or within, an aisled building. This setting of the drier 50m from the nearest building and down-wind of the presumed prevalent westerly wind may have been because of the fire risk and raises the possibility that at the present site a farm lay somewhere on the rising ground to the west or south. The most substantial heated structures having an agricultural use are those at the villas at Darenth and Keston. These were distinct from domestic room heating systems and seem designed for larger scale processing of produce than that handled in the standard separate drying oven (Philp 1973, 128; Philp *et al* 1991, 87–8). The paired ovens or driers on these two sites are similar, the heated area of each rectangular floor being between 8 and 10 square metres, that is, a combined area almost twice that of the Wainscott building. The location at one end of substantial wooden or masonry basilican barns suggests use for grain drying or malting, even if environmental evidence is lacking. The scale and pairing of ovens recalls the situation at, for instance, Rockbourne and in a recently excavated barn at Grateley, Wiltshire (Cunliffe 1999). The duplication of ovens suggests their use alternately or at different levels of heating, the oven structures and types of cereal suggesting one was run at a lower temperature and used for malting grain while the other was for drying or parching sheaves.

Other large heated structures are less certainly associated with agricultural activity. At Reculver a heated structure of unique design near the shore fort has been interpreted as a malting kiln. A floor of approximately 10 square metres overlay an extensive heated cavity fed by a series of vents from a surrounding U-shaped flue built into the thickness of the surrounding wall foundation. Whereas the Darenth and Keston structures were of chalk, tile and some flint this was of sandstone and a little tile. Evidence of use was lacking but the reported scale of burning might suggest industrial use such as a tile or pottery kiln but wasters were absent. A structure, similar in size to the Wainscott drier but with central flue flanked by two channels lined by chalk, has been identified at Springhead but there no definite furnace could be identified so use as a drier is presumed only on the basis of the plan (Penn 1968, 176–9).

Some structures identified as driers, such as rooms 121, 124 and 129 at Eccles furnished with pillared and channelled hypocausts, were probably no more than heating systems within houses (Detsicas 1972, 106). Likewise two heated rooms at the south-west corner of the main range of the Snodland villa have been identified as a corn-drier but the location and scale of the rooms suggest they were domestic rooms in one wing of the villa (Birbeck 1995, 118). At Little Chart another suite of rooms was clearly a bathing block partly decorated with mosaics (Eames 1958). An apparently isolated heated building at Highstead was similar in size to Wainscott but consisted of two rooms with pillared hypocausts heated by a furnace, the fill containing debris typical of a domestic hypocaust, the structure probably the much denuded remains of a small villa range (Tatton-Brown 1976, 236; Jenkins 2007, 95–9).

The use of small heated buildings in agricultural and industrial processes has not been much discussed other than in respect of their relative merits for drying grain or for malting (Reynolds and Langley 1979). Ethnographic parallels suggest that such buildings can have facilities to insert either a plank floor for malting or a more permeable surface, such as wickerwork and coarse cloth covers, to

allow the passage of warm gases and use for the drying or parching of crops (Monk 1987, 135). In the present case the carbonised cereal remains used in the furnace show waste from processing of cereal crops serving as fuel (p 71). The spelt wheat and small amount of barley recovered could have been from crops prepared for malting, the weed species suggesting an arable regime exploiting a range of soils. The traces of the four-poster building, Structure 2, to the north-west could suggest the presence of an adjacent raised granary on the upwind, north-western side, an area safer from the fire risk of the furnace. In a rural context, a drier of the size and quality of that at Wainscott would be more appropriate as serving a villa-sized farm, the dimensions of this building, at approximately 3.6m square, being in the upper range of such structures.

Other industrial uses can also be suggested, not all mutually exclusive, ranging from the drying of flax, the smoking of meat or fish and even the seasoning of wood (Morris 1979, 8). The presence of a drier at an Oxfordshire kiln site suggests they could have also served for the biscuit firing of pottery (Young 1977, 15–16). The presence of so much brickmaking waste in the present structure implies the presence of a kiln nearby and a connection with some aspect of the production. Although designed for agricultural use it could also have served for the careful drying of specialised and more delicate products, such as box tiles, prior to firing. While bricks and flat tile could be laid out to dry in the sun the hollow products would need care against sagging or damage while in the leather-hard state. The production of such products might have necessitated their slow drying in a warm but moist atmosphere where distortion and 'springing' of the luted joints could be prevented (I am grateful to John Walker for this suggestion, based on records of post-medieval pottery production methods, CSG). The brickyard and kiln might then lie close by, close enough for the more delicate products to be stacked within for a gentle drying process to have been carried out.

Non-industrial uses can also be suggested, particularly as small-scale bath buildings as Pitt-Rivers suggested for the small heated buildings on Cranborne Chase. That simple 'sweat-lodges' of the American Indian type existed at least in the late stages of the western Roman provinces is suggested by the description in a letter of Sidonius Apollinaris of bathing taking place in a simple wooden hut by the riverside, the main bath building being out of use at this date in the late fifth century (Sidonius Apollinaris, Letters, Book 2, 9). It is also clear from ethnographic records that structures heated for agricultural purposes could also serve as impromptu baths or sweat lodges (Barfield and Hodder 1987). Recent ethnographic accounts from Ireland and Scotland imply that although utilitarian, drying buildings also served as warm places for women and families to congregate in the course of processing cereal crops.

To summarise, the heated building may have been multi-purpose and intended for both drying and steam treating processes, whether for malting or drying grain, for drying other materials, for smoking food items or for the initial drying of box flue tiles in a controlled, steam-laden atmosphere. The building could even have served as a rudimentary steam bath. In its final stage the flues may have become unusable and were filled in with over-fired waste from a nearby tile kiln and a solid floor created; this final use cannot now be reconstructed.

Anglo-Saxon *(Period 3)*

The date of the settlement

Occupation at Wainscott appears to have ended around the early fourth century, the lack of later material suggesting a real absence of activity from the later Roman period. Although the number of finds are limited from the succeeding Period 3 this is not unusual for an Anglo-Saxon rural domestic site in Kent or, indeed, elsewhere. For settlements with post-hole buildings and few or no sunken-floored structures this is particularly the case and can be seen at similarly dated sites such as Catholme in Staffordshire (Losco-Bradley and Kinsley 2002, 10) or Maxey, Northants (Addyman 1964, 47). Although, therefore, there is some uncertainty as to the exact date of the post-Roman settlement and while much of the pottery datable to the Anglo-Saxon period was not securely stratified in deposits directly associated with the structures, it would seem likely, on the basis of the stratigraphy, ceramics (pp 43–4) and perhaps more certainly, the small finds (pp 48–53), that the main occupation was of middle Anglo-Saxon date, of the eighth and ninth centuries or slightly before. Apart from a few potentially earlier organic-tempered sherds of pottery, there is virtually no artefactual evidence for either an earlier or later phase of Anglo-Saxon occupation, and, further, the structural evidence is compatible with a Middle Saxon date. There were, for example, no sunken-floored structures, which tend to be associated with earlier Anglo-Saxon occupation sites (Andrews 1997, 21). There remain problems of absolute dating and of providing a secure chronology for the internal development of the settlement, but again this is not unusual for sites of this period and is seen at the much more densely occupied, indeed virtually urban settlement at Hamwic (Andrews 1997, 13). Much of the following discussion is therefore based on topographical factors, which include the relationship between the Anglo-Saxon features and the enclosures and structures of Period 2.

Structural evidence

The Period 3 buildings, although fragmentary, can be recognised as a form of the larger hall or barn buildings erected in the post-Roman period. Structure 3 was an example of the type with earthfast post construction and opposing doorways, its floor area of *c* 11 by 6m comparing well with other such buildings but it did not employ the elaborate and regularly spaced post settings of the more sophisticated examples at Cowdery's Down (Millett and James 1983). In this respect it is closer to buildings PG2 at Spong Hill, Norfolk and PHB3

or 4 at Mucking, Essex, both in size and the slightly irregular pattern of post-holes, although these did not have the possible internal supports which are a feature of the south-western interior of Structure 3 (Rickett 1995, 44–7, fig 60; Hamerow 1993, figs 54–5). Irregularities in the layout of the post-holes at Wainscott arose, perhaps, from the haphazard replacement of individual uprights over time and suggest a long-lived building, the associated enclosure remodelled on at least three, if not more, occasions. However, since irregularities in post-setting layout are a common occurrence in buildings of this type, it has been suggested that the use of irregular timbers in the above ground construction may be one explanation rather than haphazard replacement (Dixon 2002, 93–5).

The most unusual feature of Structure 3 however, is the bow-sided or convex nature of its long walls. Buildings of this type are relatively rare in England (no others have been found in Kent) and have been seen as being influenced by, or deriving from, specifically Viking or Scandinavian models since they occur in large numbers in some Scandinavian countries. They are now seen as part of a 'long building tradition which has a wide distribution though they are associated particularly with Viking Age Denmark' (Richards 1991, 59) and it has been suggested that it 'is no longer possible to accept the idea that houses of a convex plan were specifically Scandinavian' (Schmidt 1973, 60). Indeed, the well-known example at Bishopstone, Sussex has been dated to the fifth or sixth century, long before any Scandinavian incursion into southern Britain (Bell 1977, 202–6).

The bow-sided building at Bishopstone, which was 10m long and 4m wide is similar to Wainscott Structure 3 in its use of paired post-holes although these are much more regularly set out along the side walls, and it also had weak corners, a trait that is also perhaps evident here. It is generally considered that in these post-Roman timber buildings there is an improving structural progression through time from direct emplacement of posts in the ground, as here, through to the use of post-in-trench construction (as seen in Structure 4 below), and, finally, sill beams, and this might suggest that Structure 3 is an early example. However, this progression cannot always be demonstrated on individual sites and is not universal, so that at Brighton Hill South in Hampshire, for example, the reverse is the case, with post-hole construction predominating in later phases (Fasham *et al* 1995, 146–7). Similarly, in the seventh- to late ninth-century settlement at Flixborough, Lincolnshire there did not seem to be 'any chronological progression in the use of particular earthfast foundation styles during different phases in the occupation sequence' (Loveluck 1998, 152). It is clear that many factors can influence the type of construction or mix of traditions employed at any one site at a given time, such as ground conditions and geology, shortage or otherwise of suitable timber or the function and status of the settlement or its buildings, and perhaps something that is rarely taken into account, the intentions or proficiency of the builders themselves (Dixon 2002, 90).

In any event, bow-sided buildings of whatever type or mix of construction techniques, do not appear to be either a specifically early or late phenomenon. Thus, three of the Middle Saxon structures recorded at Hamwic and dated to the first half of the eighth century presented slightly bow-sided walls of a similar curvature to the Wainscott building (Structures 1, 15 and 29), although two of these were incomplete in plan (Andrews 1997, 50, 55). The structures were considered early examples of a vernacular tradition exemplified in later bow-sided buildings both at Hamwic and elsewhere in Hampshire (Andrews 1997, 112). This type of structure may actually be more common in middle and later Anglo-Saxon contexts, and a very late Saxon or early Norman example can be seen at Castle Rising Castle in Norfolk (Morley and Gurney 1997, 17–20), although this was only partially exposed and constructed using continuous trenches. Twelfth-century bow-sided buildings, however, which utilised single or double post-settings have also been recorded in Norfolk at North Elmham Park (Morley and Gurney 1997, 20). Although rare in relation to more rectangular or regular structures, there seems no reason to suppose that there was anything exceptional about Wainscott Structure 3 in a Middle Saxon context.

Burnt daub and charred wood in some post-holes and to the area east of Structure 3 suggested the burning of at least part of the wattle and daub superstructure of that building. Such burnt clay or daub, much of which exhibited wattle impressions, is typical of sites of the mid to later Anglo-Saxon period (Hamerow 1993, 13), but does also occur earlier.

The mixed constructional methods of the very fragmentary Structure 4 may be comparable to building A2 at Chalton, one end of which abutted a separate but linking structure A3, the construction of the two differing (Addyman et al 1972, 19–20, fig 12). The total dimensions of the two would have been similar to that proposed here. Many buildings at the Middle Saxon settlement of Hamwic however, also utilised different types of construction within the same structural unit, and this may be the case with Structure 4 (Andrews 1997, 49–50); the same can be seen at Catholme (Losco-Bradley and Kinsley 2002, 86). The open-ended nature of the structure, with only the south side delineated by a clear structural wall of mostly post-in-trench type (though the northern side may have been similarly defined), also finds parallel elsewhere, and is an indication of how the weight of the roof was almost entirely supported by the side walls in these forms of building (such as Structures 29, 45 and 46 at Hamwic; Andrews 1997, figs 49, 59, 60). In this respect, Structure 1642 at Brighton Hill South is not only open ended but its below ground arrangement is virtually identical to the main post-in-trench construction used in Structure 4 (Fasham et al 1995, 88), although it is later in date; it was interpreted as an open ended agricultural building or barn. Although the extent of Structure 4 was not fully determined and its plan ambiguous, the presence of the possible enclosure boundary or drainage gully (F115) and probably associated pit complex does suggest that another substantial domestic building existed here and the arrangement at right-angles to Structure 3 would be paralleled, for instance, in the complex of adjoining buildings A1–5 at Chalton, this group lying within an enclosure.

Enclosure 3 had passed through three changes of layout on its south and west sides and was particularly irregular in its south-western corner. These were presumably connected with increasing the enclosed area and redefining access to the north-west side of Structure 3 and the series of cess-pits enclosed by the much denuded ditches. The main group of pits was aligned to a second phase of the enclosure's south-west side and therefore post-dates its cutting. The position of the drainage gully (F115) around Structure 4 suggests its western alignment respected the north-western side of Enclosure 3, leaving a gap of 4.5m between the two. This in turn suggests that the eastern and western areas of activity are likely to have been roughly contemporary, although the central group of pits, some of which underlie and therefore pre-date Structure 4, might indicate that it was constructed later than Structure 3.

The form of enclosure systems varies considerably between contemporary sites, some, such as Chalton or Cowdery's Down on the chalk, being notable by the rarity of such features; the needs of drainage on different soils and in low-lying situations presumably partly dictated the use of such features, but other functions than drainage are possible (Hamerow 2002, 126–7). At Wainscott, ditch F326 on the eastern side of Enclosure 3 may have served a drainage function, since it was in a possibly waterlogged area and its irregular shape in plan and greater depth in comparison to the other ditches, suggest that it may have been cleaned out or recut on more regular basis (p 15).

The form and size of the enclosures surrounding the two hall-like buildings are similar to those from the sixth- to seventh-century settlement at Pennyland, Buckinghamshire (Williams 1993, 49–55). There, slight gullies or ditches outlined approximately rectangular areas, set either side of a droveway and containing hall-like buildings similar to those at Wainscott. Similar arrangements of enclosure, with subsequent enlargements can also be seen at Catholme in Staffordshire (Losco-Bradley and Kinsley 2002, 28).

The pits and their contents have been discussed above. Many of them were typologically similar to those on other Anglo-Saxon settlements, the cutting of the shafts down to the underlying gravel for drainage purposes and the poverty of cultural material in their fill being features observed elsewhere (Andrews 1997, 174; Rady 1987, 132–4; forthcoming). The pits appear to have been left open long enough for the contents to slump and later material to be deposited in the resultant hollows. This settling of the contents probably resulted from the decay of organic fills, which in some of the pits at least is likely to have been cess or other organic refuse, as suggested by the green staining, which is a common factor on various sites of the period (Andrews 1997, 175; Losco-Bradley and Kinsley 2002, 36–40). Samples from some pits confirmed the deposition of cess and some of the cleaner silt and gravel fills may have served to seal noxious layers, as at Channel Tunnel site CTF 103 (Rady forthcoming).

However, the situation may be more complex, and it is not always possible to prove the presence of cess within these features; pits F219 and F340 although exhibiting such staining and containing what were considered degraded organic deposits, did not contain unequivocal evidence for being used as cess-pits, such as mineralised faecal matter (*see* p 67). At Catholme, although the geology is different and maybe a factor, analysis of such discoloured deposits did not even show the presence of organic material (Losco-Bradley and Kinsley 2002, 36). Further, not all of the pits at Wainscott, particularly those of the western group, were of this type. It is possible therefore that the pits had some other original functions (as suggested at Hamwic; Andrews 1997, 174), perhaps even use in some industrial process such as tanning, though there is no direct evidence for such here apart from the likely organic contents of the features.

The layout, concentration and relatively large number of pits deserves some comment. Although at Hamwic many pits were apparently kept open over a long period of time, this was in a near urban context with a probably much greater population and with some pits perhaps shared between different family groups (Andrews 1997, 174). At Wainscott, it would appear that the individual pit groups were only associated with one building, and that in both groups, but particularly the eastern group, most if not all were open and perhaps in use together (p 23). Such a large group of features of such size in contemporary or near contemporary use would appear to be excessive for the simple disposal of cess from one or two family units. There is of course the possibility (see above) that the features had multifarious functions, but if, as seems likely many were for cess, the contents would have been of value as fertiliser. On some Anglo-Saxon sites the lack of pits has been explained by the fact that rubbish from the settlement was directly spread on the fields as manure (Fasham and Whinney 1991, 76), but in most cases the direct application of raw manure to crops or just before planting is deleterious. It is possible therefore, that an element of composting was involved at Wainscott, with pits emptied once the cess or other organic content had broken down and the contents then spread on the fields; other pits in the group could therefore be at different stages of this process or being actively filled. If a long life is allowed for each pit the occupation of the building adjacent to each pit group could have extended over a considerable time.

Finally, pit alignments have been noted at Hamwic, there alongside property boundaries (Andrews 1997, 179–83), and whilst the linear arrangement of the eastern pit group at Wainscott is obviously influenced by the adjacent enclosure ditch or ditches, the clear line of pits in the western group does not appear to relate to any of the identified Anglo-Saxon features. If anything, the line respects the western side of the Roman Enclosure 2, and may therefore be further evidence that this was still visible in some form. The date of the well (F300) remains problematic since on plan it lies within Enclosure 1 of the Roman period; alternatively, its proximity to Structure 4 could mean it served that building. The medieval pottery may be intrusive, the result of a collapse of a rotted timber lining at the time of the Period 4 arable land use, or even derive from the later ditch F99 which truncated it.

Cultural and environmental remains

The ceramic and other finds assemblages from Period 3 are probably too small to provide firm indications of the social status and economy of the settlement. However, apart from the Ipswich ware, all of the ceramic material was possibly locally produced, and 'in the absence of comparable Middle Saxon assemblages from the area, the overall impression is of a fairly low-status domestic settlement, isolated but with some access to coastally traded goods' (p 44). Other domestic refuse was rare but may have been placed in surface middens (Andrews 1997, 177–8) and if the primary areas of use, the buildings, were kept clean then this would account for the low level of finds from the settlement area.

Environmental material suggests normal agricultural and domestic activity including the processing of wool and weaving; sheep were possibly the most farmed animal during this period (p 62). Cereal remains from pit F141 suggest cultivation of barley, oats and rye, a range of cereals markedly different from that in the Roman heated building Structure 1, this material derived from small scale subsistence farming on a variety of sometimes poor soils to which the oats and rye would be suited. Pulses also occurred and may have been cultivated.

Some of the Anglo-Saxon features yielded small quantities of marine shell, mostly mussel. Fish bones were recovered from cess deposits within some of the pits but most of these were too fragmentary to identify to species, although vertebrae of the common eel were found in F141. Seafood obviously played some part in the diet, as might be expected of a site so close to the Medway estuary.

Evidence for industrial activity was limited to small-scale smithing, but the possibility of other industrial processes occurring within the pits remains.

Relationship to the Roman settlement

The relationship of this settlement to the latest Roman activity deserves comment in view of the limited dating evidence already outlined and especially since there are some apparent spatial relationships between Periods 2 and 3. The superimposition of a new arrangement of buildings and enclosures on a pre-existing one of late Roman date can also be paralleled at other sites; in fact it appears to be quite common. At Bishopstone (above), several buildings were excavated, part of an extensive settlement adjacent to and partly overlying a late Roman settlement enclosure (Bell 1977, 197–226). Finds from the settlement belonged to the sixth century, grave goods of a classic Anglo-Saxon type from an adjacent cemetery suggesting use of the site from the fifth to sixth centuries (*ibid*, 238–39). Elsewhere in Britain sites at Mucking, West Stow and Spong Hill have likewise produced early Anglo-Saxon settlements with hall houses and/or sunken-floored buildings and enclosures superimposed on a previous Romano-British landscape (Hamerow 1993; West 1985, fig 7; Rickett 1995, figs 144–45).

These sites are earlier than Wainscott, but the evidence suggests that the late third-century Roman enclosures were still visible by the time the site was reoccupied, perhaps during the seventh century, and perhaps influenced its arrangement (such a scenario has also been postulated for Dolland's Moor near Folkestone; Rady forthcoming). Firstly, apart from the western pit group, all of the exposed Anglo-Saxon features are confined within the large Roman Enclosure 2 (although further north of the examined area the situation could be different) with elements of the Enclosure 3 ditches, respecting the position of the south-western side of the enclosure; the central length of Enclosure 3 ditch F127 was also parallel to the western side of Enclosure 2, which may be more than coincidence. Further, the western pit group seems to be arranged in a way that reflects the Roman alignments suggesting that the features may have been purposefully situated immediately outside of the remnant Roman enclosure, and again that its ditch and perhaps a bank were still evident. However, the arrangement of Enclosure 3 and the structures and directly associated features, shows that by this stage the alignment of the site had been shifted by 45 degrees to the east

A new entrance-way into the area was formed in the southern corner of Enclosure 3, directly over the Roman ditch, for reasons which are not readily clear. There are however, some topographical indications that there was also access from the west, and that the entrance of Enclosure 2, perhaps still delineated by remnant but mostly infilled ditches, continued to serve as a causeway. Here, the entrance gave access to an open area on the right, in the south-western corner of the enclosure, but also led to an open strip 4m wide which continued east for a distance of 20m before turning north-east and continuing beyond the limits of excavation. This route was respected in both periods, Structures 1 and its successor (4) lying on one side, Enclosure 3 lying on the other. The first phase of Enclosure 3 would allow access up to the north-west side of Structure 3, pits F131 and F141 lying either side of the access. In the second phase this route was blocked by F127 but in the third and fourth the route was re-opened, F25 and F324 flanking its southern side.

The Anglo-Saxon settlement in its Kentish context

This is one of the few rural settlements of the period to have been excavated in western Kent apart from sunken-floored buildings at Keston and St Mary Cray; (Philp 1973, 156–9; Hart 1984). Survey of sites in the Darent valley has, however, identified not only a series of cemeteries but settlement traces, often in close proximity to known Roman villa sites (Tyler 1992, 79–80). In Kent as a whole, rural settlements of this period have rarely been identified but similar earthfast timber buildings, in association with sunken-floored structures have been identified at Church Whitfield (Parfitt 1997, 29–30).

Further settlement, including traces of structures, has also been examined at Harrietsham (Jarman 2002, 17), on the Isle of Thanet (Hutcheson and Andrews 1997), and in the Folkestone area (Rady forthcoming). None however are morphologically similar to the Middle Saxon occupation located at Wainscott, and, moreover, are mostly from the earlier Anglo-Saxon period: the site therefore remains unique for Kent at the time of writing. It is therefore difficult at the moment to relate this particular site to the overall nature of Anglo-Saxon rural occupation in western Kent or Kent as a whole.

Medieval and post-medieval *(Period 4)*

After the abandonment or destruction of the Period 3 settlement a period of perhaps 200 years passed before evidence for arable strip farming could be identified. The pottery associated with these features does not appear to be derived from any *in situ* occupation and must be from elsewhere, though the concentration of material is rather surprising and is suggestive of early medieval occupation not too far away. Ridge and furrow, the common form of cultivation of the medieval period, has been extensively studied but the individual selions or strips making up the furlongs were thought not to be separated by any form of boundary, other than that which might be formed by years of ploughing (Beresford and St Joseph 1958, 25). At Wainscott, however, the presence of parallel ditches, albeit over only a small area, do suggest separation into strips marked by shallow ditches possibly because of the low-lying situation and poor drainage. These strips were, by all accounts, 5.5 yards wide, similar to the distance recorded here. It is possible that part of a similar system was exposed at Saltwood, a series of parallel ditches 5–6m apart being identified there and dated approximately to the early medieval period (Willson 2002, 38).

During the period of this agricultural land use the site lay within the parish of Frindsbury. The place name of Wainscott, if interpreted literally, refers to a small settlement or even a single dwelling of a carter. The agricultural use of the land in the early medieval period cannot be linked to any particular settlement or farm; in recent times the nearest farms are Islingham Farm, 500m to the north-west and Blacklands 800m to the west. The lack of archaeological evidence over the remainder of the route of the Wainscott northern by-pass may suggest an absence of significant past settlement in this area. The uninhabited nature of the place, at least in the medieval period, may be confirmed by Shakespeare's setting in Scene 2 Act I of the First Part of Henry IV of a highway robbery at Gads Hill which was also the site of a number of similar events in later centuries (Richard Cross, pers comm). Such incidents seem inconceivable with the density of present day settlement and the level of activity on the present road system.

Bibliography

Addyman, P 1964, 'A Dark-Age Settlement at Maxey, Northants', *Medieval Archaeology* 8, 20–73

Addyman, P 1973, 'Late Saxon settlements in the St Neots area: III, the village or township at St Neots [Huntingdon and Peterborough]', *Proceedings of the Cambridgeshire Antiquarian Society* 64, 45–99

Addyman, P and Hill, D 1969, 'Saxon Southampton – a review of the evidence: Part I, history, location, date and character of the town', *Proceedings of the Hampshire Field Club Archaeological Society* 25, 61–93

Addyman, P, Leigh, D and Hughes, M 1972, 'Anglo-Saxon houses at Chalton, Hants', *Medieval Archaeology* 16, 13–32

Andrews, G 1985, *Archaeology of Canterbury: an Assessment*, HBMC(E), London

Andrews, P (ed) 1997, *Excavations at Hamwic: Volume 2: excavations at Six Dials*, Council for British Archaeology Research Report 109, York

Armitage, P and Chapman, H 1979, 'Roman mules', *London Archaeologist* 3, 339–46

Arnold, A 1887, 'Roman remains and celt found near Quarry House, Frindsbury', *Archaeologia Cantiana* xvii, 189–92

Arnold, A 1889, 'On Roman remains found in Frindsbury', *Archaeologia Cantiana* xviii, 189–92

Astill, G and Lobb, S 1989, 'Excavation of prehistoric, Roman, and Saxon deposits at Wraysbury, Berkshire', *Archaeological Journal* cxlvi, 68–134

Barfield, L and Hodder, M 1987, 'Burnt mounds as saunas and the prehistory of bathing', *Antiquity* 61, 370–9

Baxter I 1998, 'Species identification of equids from Western European archaeological deposits: methodologies, techniques and problems' in S Anderson and K Boyle (eds), *Current and Recent Research in Osteoarchaeology*, Oxford: Oxbow Books, 3–17

Bell, M 1977, 'Excavations at Bishopstone, East Sussex [Rookery Hill]', *Sussex Archaeological Collections* 115, 83–117

Bendrey, R 1999, 'A note on the identification of donkey (*Equus asinus* L) bones from Roman Southwark', *Organ* 22, 7–12

Bendrey, R 2007, 'The development of new methodologies for studying the horse: case studies from prehistoric southern England', PhD thesis, University of Southampton

Bendrey, R 2008, 'The animal bone' in Hicks 2008, 233–62

Bennett, P 1978, '77–79 Castle Street, Canterbury. Stage II', *Archaeologia Cantiana* xciv, 275–6

Bennett, P, Frere, S and Stow, S 1982, *Excavations at Canterbury Castle*, The Archaeology of Canterbury I, Maidstone: Kent Archaeological Society for Canterbury Archaeological Trust

Bennett, P, Clark, P, Hicks, A, Rady, J and Riddler I 2008, *At the Great Crossroads: Prehistoric, Roman and medieval discoveries on the Isle of Thanet 1994–95*, Canterbury Archaeological Trust Occasional Paper no 4, Canterbury

Bennett, P, Riddler, I and Sparey-Green, C forthcoming *The Roman Watermills and Settlement at Ickham, near Canterbury Kent*, The Archaeology of Canterbury (New Series) V

Beresford, M and St Joseph, J 1958, *Medieval England, An Aerial Survey*, 2nd edition, Cambridge University Press

Betts, I M 1992, 'Roman tile from Eccles, Kent found at Colchester' in P Crummy (ed), *Excavations at Culver Street, The Gilberd School and other sites in Colchester 1971–85*, Colchester Archaeological Trust Report 6, Colchester: Colchester Archaeological Trust, 259–60

Biddle, M (ed) 1990, *Object and economy in medieval Winchester, (Artefacts from medieval Winchester part ii)*, Winchester Studies 7(ii), Oxford: Oxford University Press

Birbeck, V 1995, 'Excavations on a Romano-British villa at Churchfields, Snodland 1992–4', *Archaeologia Cantiana* cxv, 71–120

Bishop, M 1996, *Finds from Roman Aldborough: A Catalogue of Small Finds from the Romano-British Town of Isurium Brigantum*, Oxford: Oxbow Monograph 65

Blackmore, L 2001, 'The imported and non-local Saxon pottery' in M Gardiner *et al*, 192–207

Blinkhorn, P forthcoming, *The Ipswich Ware Project: Ceramics, Trade and Society in Middle Saxon England*, Medieval Pottery Research Group Special Paper

Blockley, K, Blockley, M, Blockley, P, Frere, S and Stow, S 1995, *Excavations in the Marlowe Car Park and Surrounding Areas*, The Archaeology of Canterbury V, Whitstable: Canterbury Archaeological Trust

Boardman, S and Jones, G 1990, 'Experiments on the effects of charring on cereal plant components', *Journal of Archaeological Science* 17/1, 1–12

Boessneck, J 1969, 'Osteological differences between sheep (*Ovis aries* Linné) and goat (*Capra hircus* Linné)' in D Brothwell and E Higgs (eds), *Science in Archaeology*, London: Thames and Hudson, 331–58

Bordes, F 1961, *Typologie du Paléolithique ancien et moyen*, 2 vols, Mémoires de l'Institut Préhistoriques de l'Université de Bordeaux 1, Bordeaux: Delmas

Bowen, H 1990, *The Archaeology of Bokerley Dyke*, London: HMSO

Bridgland, D 1998, *The Pleistocene History and Early Human Occupation of the River Thames Valley Stone Age Archaeology: Essays in Honour of John Wymer*, Oxford: Oxbow Books

Brodribb, A, Hands, A and Walker, D 1968, *Excavations [of Roman villa complex] at Shakenoak [Oxon]: I, Sites A and D*, Oxford: Exeter College

Brodribb, A, Hands, A and Walker, D 1971, *Excavations at Shakenoak Farm, near Wilcote, Oxfordshire: Part II, Sites B and H*, Omega Press

Brodribb, A, Hands, A and Walker, D 1972, *Excavations at Shakenoak Farm [Roman–early Anglo-Saxon site] near Wilcote, Oxfordshire: III, Site F*, Oxford: Exeter College

Brodribb, G 1987, *Roman Brick and Tile*, London: Alan Sutton

Butler, C 2000, *Saxon Settlement and Earlier Remains at Friars Oak, Hassocks, West Sussex*, British Archaeological Reports (British Series) 295, Oxford

Campbell, G 1994, 'The preliminary archaeobotanical results from Anglo-Saxon West Cotton and Raunds' in J Rackham (ed), *Environment and Economy in Anglo-Saxon England*, Council for British Archaeology Research Report 89, 65–82

Catherall, P 1983, 'A Romano-British pottery manufacturing site at Oakleigh Farm, Higham, Kent', *Britannia* xiv, 103–42

Clapham, A, Tutin, T and Moore, D 1989, *Flora of the British Isles*, Cambridge: Cambridge University Press

Clark K 1995, 'The later prehistoric and protohistoric dog: the emergence of canine diversity', *Archaeozoologia* 7/2, 9–32

Clark, J, Higgs, E and Longworth, I 1960, 'Excavations at the Neolithic site at Hurst Fen, Mildenhall, Suffolk, 1954, 1957 and 1958', *Proceedings of the Prehistoric Society* xxvi, 202–45

Clarke, G 1979, *Winchester studies 3: pre-Roman and Roman Winchester – part 2, the Roman cemetery at Lankhills*, Oxford: Clarendon Press

Clutton-Brock, J 1992, *Horse Power*, London: Natural History Museum Publications

Cook, N 1936, 'Archaeology in Kent, 1936', *Archaeologia Cantiana* xlviii, 234–5

Corder, P 1954, *The Roman town and villa at Great Casterton, Rutland: Second interim Report 1951–3*, University of Nottingham

Corder, P 1961, *The Roman town and villa at Great Casterton, Rutland: Third report for the years 1954–1958*, University of Nottingham

Couldrey, P 2003, 'Prehistoric pottery' in P Hutchings, 'Ritual and riverside settlement: a multi-period site at Princes Road, Dartford', *Archaeologia Cantiana* cxxiii, 41–69

Courty, M, Goldberg, G and Macphail, R 1989, *Soils and micromorphology in archaeology*, Cambridge University Press

Cowie, R, Whytehead, R and Blackmore, L 1988, 'Two Middle Saxon occupation sites: excavations at Jubilee Hall and 21–22 Maiden Lane', *Transactions of the London and Middlesex Archaeological Society* 39, 47–163

Crummy, N (ed) 1983, *The Roman small finds from excavations in Colchester 1971–9*, Colchester Archaeological Reports 2, Colchester

Cruse, R 1987, 'Further investigation of the Acheulian site at Cuxton', *Archaeologia Cantiana* civ, 39–81

Cunliffe, B 1999, *Grately South Excavation 1999 Interim Report*, The Danebury Environs Roman Project, The Danebury Trust and Institute of Archaeology, Oxford

Dacre, M and Ellison, A 1981, 'A Bronze Age urn cemetery at Kimpton, Hampshire', *Proceedings of the Prehistoric Society* xlvii, 147–203

Dannell, G and Wild, J 1987, *Longthorpe II. The Military Works-Depot: An Episode in Landscape History*, Britannia Monograph Series 8, London

Detsicas A 1972, 'Excavations at Eccles 1971, Tenth Interim Report', *Archaeologia Cantiana* lxxxvii, 101–10

Dixon, P 2002, 'The reconstruction of the buildings' in S Losco-Bradley and G Kinsley, 89–99

Dobney, K and Reilly, K 1988, 'A method for recording archaeological animal bones: the use of diagnostic zones', *Circaea* 5/1, 79–96

Eames, J 1958, 'A Roman bath-house at Little Chart, Kent', *Archaeologia Cantiana* lxxi, 130–46

Eisenmann, V 1986, 'Comparative osteology of modern and fossil horses, half-asses, and asses' in R Meadow and H-P Uerpmann (eds), *Equids in the Ancient World*, Wiesbaden, 67–116

Evison, V 1987, *Dover: the Buckland Anglo-Saxon cemetery*, London: HBMC Archaeological Reports 3

Fasham, P and Whinney, R 1991, *Archaeology and the M3*, Hampshire Field Club Monograph 7

Fasham, P, Keevil, G and Coe, D 1995, *Brighton Hill South (Hatch Warren): an Iron Age Farmstead and Deserted Medieval Village in Hampshire*, Wessex Archaeological Reports 7

Frere, S 1972, Verulamium Excavations: Volume I, Report of the Research Committee of the Society of Antiquaries of London 28, Oxford

Frere, S 1984, *Verulamium Excavations: Volume III*, Oxford University Committee for Archaeology Monograph 1, Oxford

Gardiner, M, Cross, R, Macpherson-Grant, N and Riddler, I 2001, 'Continental trade and non-urban ports in Mid-Anglo-Saxon England: Excavations at Sandtun, West Hythe, Kent', *Archaeological Journal* clviii, 161–290

Godwin, H 1975, *The history of the British flora: a factual basis for phytogeography*, Cambridge University Press (2nd edition)

Grant, A 1982, 'The use of tooth wear as a guide to the age of domestic ungulates' in B Wilson *et al*, 91–108

Grant, A 1988, 'Animal resources' in G Astill and A Grant (eds), *The Countryside of Medieval England*, Oxford: Blackwell, 149–87

Grant, A 1989, 'Animals in Roman Britain' in M Todd (ed), *Research in Roman Britain 1960–1989*, Britannia Monograph Series 11, 135–46

Green, C and Rollo-Smith, S 1984, 'The excavation of eighteen round barrows near Shrewton, Wiltshire', *Proceedings of the Prehistoric Society* 50, 255–312

Green, F 1991, 'Landscape archaeology in Hampshire: the Saxon Plant Remains' in J Renfrew (ed), *New Light on Early Farming*, Edinburgh University Press, 363–78

Green, M 1976, *A corpus of Religious Material from the Civilian Areas of Roman Britain*, British Archaeological Reports (British Series) 24, Oxford

Grigson, C 1982, 'Sex and age determination of some bones and teeth of domestic cattle: review of the literature' in B Wilson *et al*, 7–23

Haio Zimmermann, W 1978, 'Economy of the Roman Iron Age settlement at Flögeln, Kr Cuxhaven: Lower Saxony husbandry, cattle farming and manufacturing' in B Cunliffe and T Rowley, *Lowland Iron Age Communities in Europe*, British Archaeological Reports (International Series) 48, Oxford

Halstead, P 1985, 'A study of mandibular teeth from Romano-British contexts at Maxey' in F Pryor, C French, D Crowther, D Gurney, G Simpson and M Taylor (eds), *Archaeology and Environment in the Lower Welland Valley Volume 1*, East Anglian Archaeology 27, 219–24

Hambleton, E 1999, *Animal Husbandry Regimes in Iron Age Britain: a comparative study of faunal assemblages from British Iron Age sites*, British Archaeological Reports (British Series) 282, Oxford

Hamerow, H 1993, *Excavations at Mucking: Volume 2: The Anglo-Saxon Settlement*, English Heritage Archaeological Reports 21, London

Hamerow, H 2002, 'Catholme: The development and context of the settlement' in S Losco-Bradley and G Kinsley, 123–9

Harcourt, R 1974, 'The dog in prehistoric and early historic Britain', *Journal of Archaeological Science* 1, 151–76

Hart, F 1984, 'Evidence of a Saxon Grubenhaus and Roman ditch at Kent Road, St Mary Cray', *Archaeologia Cantiana* ci, 187–216

Hawkes, S and Hogarth, A 1974, 'The Anglo-Saxon Cemetery at Monkton, Thanet', *Archaeologia Cantiana* lxxxix, 49–89

Hicks, A 2008, 'The Roman Settlement' in P Bennett *et al*, 101–278

Hillman, G 1981, 'Reconstructing crop husbandry practices from charred remains of crops' in R Mercer (ed), *Farming Practice in British Prehistory*, (2nd ed) Edinburgh: University Press

Hillman, G 1982, 'Evidence for spelting malt' in R Leech (ed), 137–41

Hillman, G 1994, 'Interpretation of archaeological plant remains: the application of ethnographic models from Turkey' in W van Zeist and W Casparie (eds), *Plants and Ancient Man: Studies in Palaeoethnobotany*, Rotterdam: A A Balkema, 43–69

Hinton, D 1996, *The Gold, Silver and other Non-Ferrous Alloy Objects from Hamwic, Southampton Finds Volume Two*, Southampton Archaeology Monographs 6, Stroud

Hutcheson, A and Andrews, P 1997, *Excavations at a Late Bronze Age, Anglo-Saxon and Medieval Settlement Site at Manston Road, Ramsgate, 1995–7; Draft Report*, unpunlished client report, Wessex Archaeology

James, S, Marshall, A and Millett, M 1984, 'An early medieval building tradition', *Archaeological Journal* cxli, 182–215

Jarman, C 2002, 'Glebeland, Marley Road, Harrietsham', *Canterbury's Archaeology 1997–1998*, Canterbury Archaeological Trust, 16–17

Jenkins, F 1956, 'A Roman tilery and two pottery kilns at *Durovernum* (Canterbury)', *Antiquaries Journal* xxxvi, 40–56

Jenkins, F 1960, 'Two pottery kilns and a tilery of the Roman period at Canterbury (*Durovernum Cantiacorum*)', *Archaeologia Cantiana* lxxiv, 151–61

Jenkins, F 2007, 'The hypocausted building' in Bennett, P, Couldrey, P and Macpherson-Grant, N, *Highstead, near Chislet, Kent: Excavations 1975–1977*, Archaeology of Canterbury (New Series) IV, Broadstairs, Canterbury Archaeological Trust, 95–9

Jessup, R 1930, *The Archaeology of Kent*, Methuen County Archaeology Series

Johnston, D 1972, 'A Roman building at Chalk, near Gravesend', *Britannia* iii, 112–48

Kelly, D 1987, 'Archaeological notes from Maidstone Museum: Frindsbury', *Archaeologia Cantiana* civ, 350–1

Lakin, D 1999, A Romano-British site at Summerton Way, Thamesmead, London Borough of Bexley', *Archaeologia Cantiana* cxix, 311–42

Leech, R (ed) 1982, *Excavations at Catsgore 1970–1973, A Romano-British Village*, Western Archaeological Trust Excavation Monograph No 2, Bristol

Lethbridge, T 1936, *A Cemetery at Shudy Camps, Cambridgeshire*, Cambridge Antiquarian Society Quarto Publications, New Series 5, Cambridge

Letts, J 2000, 'Charred plant remains' in J Pine, 'The excavation of medieval and post-medieval features at the rear of 42c Bell Street, Henley, Oxfordshire', *Oxoniensia* 64, 255–74, 269

Levine, M 1982, 'The use of crown height measurements and eruption-wear sequences to age horse teeth' in B Wilson *et al*, 223–350

Losco-Bradley, S and Kinsley, G 2002, *Catholme: An Anglo-Saxon Settlement on the Trent Gravels in Staffordshire*, Nottingham Studies in Archaeology Volume 3

Loveluck, C 1998, 'A high-status Anglo-Saxon settlement at Flixborough, Lincolnshire', *Antiquity* 72/275, 146–61

Lucas, R 1993, *The Romano-British villa at Halstock, Dorset, Excavations 1967–1985*, Dorset Natural History and Archaeological Society monograph 13

MacGregor, A and Bolick, E 1993, *Ashmolean Museum, Oxford: A Summary Catalogue of the Anglo-Saxon Collections (Non-Ferrous Metals)*, British Archaeological Reports (British Series) 230, Oxford

Macpherson-Grant, N 1995, 'Post-Roman Pottery' in K Blockley *et al*, 815–920

Macpherson-Grant, N 2001, 'The Local Saxon and Later Pottery' in M Gardiner *et al*, 208–25

Macpherson-Grant, N, Savage, A, Cotter, J, Davey, M, and Riddler, I 1995, *Canterbury Ceramics 2*, Canterbury Archaeological Trust

Malim, T and Hines, J 1998, *The Anglo-Saxon cemetery at Edix Hill (Barrington A), Cambridgeshire: excavations 1989–1991 and a summary catalogue of material from 19th century interventions*, Council for British Archaeology Research Report 112, York

Mann, J 1982, *Early Medieval Finds from Flaxengate I: Objects of antler, bone, stone, horn, ivory, amber and jet*, The Archaeology of Lincoln 14/1, London

Manning, W 1985, *Catalogue of the Romano-British iron tools, fittings and weapons in the British Museum*, London

Manning, W, Price, J and Webster, J 1995, *Report on the Excavations at Usk 1965–76: The Roman Small Finds*, Cardiff: University of Wales Press

Markham, G 1681, *A Way to Get Wealth*, London

Mayer, J and Brisbin, I 1988, 'Sex identification of *Sus scrofa* based on canine morphology', *Journal of Mammalogy* 69/2, 408–12

Meaney, A 1964, *A Gazetteer of Early Anglo-Saxon Burial Sites*, London

Meates, G 1987, *The Roman villa at Lullingstone, Kent, Volume II: The wall paintings and finds*, Kent Archaeological Society monograph series 3, Maidstone

Miles, D (ed) 1986, *Archaeology at Barton Court Farm, Abingdon, Oxon: an investigation of late Neolithic, Iron Age, Romano-British, and Saxon settlements*, Oxford Archaeological Unit Report 3, Council For British Archaeology Research Report 50, London

Millet, M and James, S 1983, 'Excavations at Cowdery's Down, Basingstoke, Hampshire, 1978–81', *Archaeological Journal* cxl, 151–279

Milne, G and Richards, J 1992, *Wharram: A Study of Settlement on the Yorkshire Wolds, VII. Two Anglo-Saxon Buildings and Associated Finds*, York University Archaeological Publications 9

Monaghan, J 1987, *Upchurch and Thameside Roman Pottery: A ceramic typology for northern Kent, first to third centuries AD*, British Archaeological Reports (British Series) 173, Oxford

Monk, M 1987, 'Archaeobotanical Studies at Poundbury' in C Sparey-Green, *Excavations at Poundbury, Volume 1: The Settlements*, Dorset Natural History and Archaeological Society Monograph 7, Dorchester, 132–7

Morley, B and Gurney, D 1997, *Castle Rising Castle, Norfolk*, East Anglian Archaeology 81, Gressenhall

Morris, P 1979, *Agricultural Buildings in Roman Britain*, British Archaeological Reports (British Series) 70, Oxford

Murphy, P 1985, 'The plant remains' in M Atkin, A Carter and D Evans, *Excavations in Norwich 1971–78, Part II*, East Anglian Archaeology 26, 144–273

Musty, J and Manning, W 1977, 'A wooden chest from the Roman villa at Bradwell, Milton Keynes, Bucks', *Antiquaries Journal* lvii, 330–2

Myres, J and Green, B 1973, *The Anglo-Saxon cemeteries of Caistor-by-Norwich and Markshall, Norfolk*, Society of Antiquaries of London Research Report 30, London

Neal, D, Wardle, A, and Hunn, J 1990, *Excavation of the Iron Age, Roman and medieval settlement at Gorhambury, St Albans*, English Heritage Archaeological Report 14, HBMC: Norwich

Needham, S 1996, 'Chronology and periodisation in the British Bronze Age', *Acta Archaeologica* 67, 121–40

O'Connor, T 1985, 'On quantifying vertebrates: some sceptical observations', *Circaea* 3, 27–30

Orton, C 1975, 'Quantitative pottery studies, some progress, problems and prospects', *Science and Archaeology* 16, 30–5

Parfitt, K 1997, 'Site 2: Church Whitfield cross-roads', *Canterbury's Archaeology 1995–1996*, Canterbury Archaeological Trust, 29–31

Parfitt, K and Brugmann, B 1997, *The Anglo-Saxon Cemetery at Mill Hill, Deal*, London: Society for Medieval Archaeology Monograph 14

Payne, S 1973, 'Kill-off patterns in sheep and goats: The Mandibles from Aşvan Kale', *Anatolian Studies* 23, 281–303

Payne, S 1985, 'Morphological distinctions between the mandibular teeth of young sheep, *Ovis*, and goats, *Capra*', *Journal of Archaeological Science* 12, 139–47

Peacock, D 1980, 'The Roman millstone trade: a petrological sketch', *World Archaeology* 12, 43–53

Pearson, E and Robinson, M 1994, 'Environmental evidence from the villa' in R Williams and R Zeepvat, *Bancroft, A Late Bronze Age Settlement, Roman Villa and Temple Mausoleum*, Aylesbury: Buckinghamshire Archaeological Society Monograph 7, 565–84

Peers, C and Radford, C 1943, 'The Saxon Monastery of Whitby', *Archaeologia* 89, 27–8

Pelling, R 2001, 'The charred plant remains' in A Hardy, *Excavations at Northfleet Substation*, Oxford Archaeology Occasional Paper, 33–7

Penn, K 1968, 'Springhead: Miscellaneous Excavations', *Archaeologia Cantiana* lxxxiii, 163–92

Philp, B 1973, *Excavations in West Kent 1960–1970*, Second Research Report in the Kent Monograph Series, Dover

Philp, B 1981, *The excavation of the Roman forts of the Classis Britannia at Dover, 1970–1977*, Third research report in the Kent monograph series, Dover

Philp, B, Parfitt, K, Willson, J, Dutto, M and Williams, W 1991, *The Roman Villa site at Keston, Kent*, First Report on Excavations 1968–78, Dover

Pitt-Rivers, A L F 1887, *Excavation in Cranborne Chase near Rushmore on the borders of Dorset and Wiltshire Volume 1*, London

Pollard, R 1988, *The Roman Pottery of Kent*, Kent Archaeological Society Monograph, 5

Pratt, S and Newstead, J 1997, 'Wainscott Northern Link: Archaeological Evaluation', unpublished report, Canterbury Archaeological Trust and Royal Holloway College

Prummel, W and Frisch, H-J 1986, 'A guide for the distinction of species, sex and body side in bones of sheep and goat', *Journal of Archaeological Science* 13, 567–77

Rady, J 1987, 'Excavations at St Martin's Hill, Canterbury 1984–85', *Archaeologia Cantiana* civ, 123–218

Rady, J forthcoming, 'The Archaeology of the Channel Tunnel Terminal at Cheriton, Folkestone, 1987–1992'

Rady, J, Allison, E, Davey, M, Harrison, L, Holmes, T, Linklater, A, Macpherson-Grant, N, Riddler, I, Savage, A, Sparey-Green, C and Ward, A 2000, *Archaeological work along the route of the Wainscott Northern By-pass and at Four Elms Roundabout 1992–1997*, unpublished archive report, Canterbury Archaeological Trust

Reynolds P and Langley J 1979, 'Romano-British corn-drying oven: an experiment', *Archaeological Journal* cxxxvi, 27–42

Richards, J 1991, *Viking Age England*, London: English Heritage Series, Batsford

Richards, J 1999, 'Cottam: an Anglian and Anglo-Scandinavian settlement on the Yorkshire Wolds', *Archaeological Journal* clvi, 1–110

Richards, J 2000, 'Anglo-Saxon settlements and archaeological visibility in the Yorkshire Wolds' in H Geake and J Kenny (eds), *Early Deira: Archaeological studies of the East Riding in the fourth to ninth centuries AD*, Oxbow Books, 27–39

Rickett, R 1995, *The Anglo-Saxon Cemetery at Spong Hill, North Elmham, Part VII, The Iron Age, Roman and Early Saxon Settlement*, East Anglian Archaeology 73, Dereham, Norfolk

Riddler, I 1999, 'The Small Finds' in M Houliston, 'Excavations at The Mount Roman Villa, Maidstone, 1994', *Archaeologia Cantiana* cxix, 71–172

Riddler, I 2008a, 'Querns' in P Bennett *et al* 203–11

Riddler, I 2008b, 'Agricultural implements' in P Bennett *et al*, 215–19

Riha, E 1986, *Römisches Toilettgerät und medizinische Instrumente aus Augst und Kaiseraugst*, Augst: Forschungen in Augst, Band 6

Roe, D 1968, 'British Lower and Middle Palaeolithic handaxe groups', *Proceedings of the Prehistoric Society* 34, 1–82

Rogers, N 1993, *Anglian and other Finds from Fishergate*, The Archaeology of York, 17/9, London

Rogerson, A and Dallas, C 1984, *Excavations in Thetford 1948–59 and 1973–80*, East Anglian Archaeology 22, Norfolk Archaeological Unit

Saville, A 1980, 'On the measurement of struck flakes and flake tools', *Lithic Studies Society Newsletter* 1, 16–20

Schmid, E 1972, *Atlas of animal bones for prehistorians, archaeologists and quaternary geologists*, Amsterdam: Elsevier

Schmidt, H 1973, 'The Trelleborg House Reconsidered', *Medieval Archaeology* 17, 52–77

Scull, C 1992, 'Excavations and survey at Watchfield, Oxfordshire, 1983–92', *Archaeological Journal* cxlix, 124–281

Silver, I 1969, 'The ageing of domestic animals' in D Brothwell and E Higgs (eds), *Science and Archaeology*, London: Thames and Hudson, 250–68

Silverside, A 1977, *A phytosociological survey of British arable-weed and related communities*, PhD Thesis, University of Durham

Stamper, P and Croft, R 2000, *Wharram: A Study of Settlement in the Yorkshire Wolds VIII: The South Manor Area*, York University Archaeological Publications 10

Sumner, H 1913, *The Ancient Earthworks of Cranborne Chase,* London: Chiswick Press

Tatton-Brown, T 1976, 'Highstead, Near Chislet', *Archaeologia Cantiana* xvii, 236–8

Taylor, M 1932, 'Romano-British Remains and Country Houses', *Victoria County History* 3, 102–26

Taylor, M, Jessup, R and Hawkes C 1932, 'Topographical Index', *Victoria County History* 3, 144–76

Tester, P 1961, 'The Roman Villa in Cobham Park near Rochester', *Archaeologia Cantiana* lxxvi, 30–60

Tester, P 1965, 'An Acheulian Site at Cuxton', *Archaeologia Cantiana* lxxx, 30–60

Thornhill, P and Payne, P 1980, 'Some sites in North Kent', *Archaeologia Cantiana* xcvi, 378–82

Tyler, S 1992, 'Anglo-Saxon Settlement in the Darent Valley and Environs', *Archaeologia Cantiana* cx, 71–81

Union Rail Limited 1999, *Thurnham Roman Villa, Thurnham, Kent ARC THM 98, Detailed Archaeological Works, Interim Report (Final)*, Oxford Archaeological Unit

Vallance, A 1920, 'Research and Discoveries in Kent', *Archaeologia Cantiana* xxxiv, 158

van der Veen, M 1989, 'National wheat-growing experiment: interim report 1987/8', *Circaea* 6, 71–6

von den Driesch, A 1976, *A Guide to the Measurement of Animal Bones from Archaeological Sites*, Cambridge, Mass: Harvard University Press

von den Driesch, A and Boessneck, J 1974, 'Kritische Anmerkungen zur Wiederisthoherberechnung aus Längenmassen vor- und frühgeschichtlicher Tierknocken', *Saugetierkundliche Mitteilungen* 22, 325–48

Wallenberg, J 1931, *Kentish Placenames*, Uppsala

Walton Rogers, P 1997, *Textile Production at 16–22 Coppergate*, The Archaeology of York: The Small Finds 17/11, London

Ward, A 1992, 'Wainscott Northern By-pass: Archaeological Ground Survey: January 1992', unpublished Canterbury Archaeological Trust client report

Ward, A 1994a 'Two 'watching brief' projects on the line of the Medway Northern Link', unpublished Canterbury Archaeological Trust client report

Ward, A 1994b, 'A 'watching brief' along the Wainscott gas pipeline', unpublished Canterbury Archaeological Trust client report 1994/25/1

West, S 1985, *West Stow: The Anglo-Saxon Village*, East Anglian Archaeology 24, Ipswich

Wheatley, S 1926, 'Find of flint instruments and workshop at Frindsbury' in Notes and Discoveries, *Archaeologia Cantiana* xxxviii, 183–4

Whytehead, R, Cowie, R and Blackmore, L 1989, 'Excavations at the Peabody site, Chandos Place, and the National Gallery', *Transactions of the London and Middlesex Archaeological Society* 40, 35–176

Williams, F 1979, *Excavations on Marefair, Northampton, 1977*, Northamptonshire Archaeology 14

Williams, R 1993, *Pennyland and Hartigans: Two Iron Age and Saxon Sites in Milton Keynes*, Buckinghamshire Archaeology Society Monograph Series 4

Willson, J 2002, 'Land north of Saltwood Tunnel', *Canterbury's Archaeology* 1999–2000, Canterbury Archaeological Trust, 35–38

Wilmott, T, Hird, L, Izzard, K and Summerfield, J 1997, *Birdoswald, excavations of a Roman fort on Hadrian's Wall and its successor settlements 1987–92*, English Heritage Archaeological Report 14

Wilson, B, Grigson, C and Payne, S (eds) 1982, *Ageing and Sexing Animal Bones from Archaeological Sites*, British Archaeological Reports (British Series) 109, Oxford

Wrathmell, S and Nicholson, A (eds) 1990, *Dalton Parlours Iron Age Settlement and Roman Villa*, Yorkshire Archaeology 3

Wymer, J 1985, *Palaeolithic Sites of East Anglia*, Norwich: Geo Books

Young, C 1977, *The Roman Pottery Industry of the Oxford Region*, British Archaeological Reports (British Series) 43, Oxford

Index